HURRAH FOR HAMPTON!

HURRAH FOR HAMPTON!

BLACK RED SHIRTS IN SOUTH CAROLINA DURING RECONSTRUCTION

Edmund L. Drago

THE UNIVERSITY OF ARKANSAS PRESS
FAYETTEVILLE 1998

Manufactured in the United States of America

02 01 00 99 98 5 4 3 2 1

Designer: Chiquita Babb

♾ The paper used in this publication meets the minimum requirements of the American National Standard for Permanence of Paper for Printed Library Materials Z39.48-1984.

Library of Congress Cataloging-in-Publication Data

Drago, Edmund L.

Hurrah for Hampton! : Black Red Shirts in South Carolina during Reconstruction / Edmund L. Drago

p. cm.

Includes bibliographical references (p.) and index.

ISBN 1-55728-541-1 (cloth : alk. paper)

1. Afro-Americans—South Carolina—Politics and government. 2. Hampton, Wade, 1818–1902. 3. South Carolina—Politics and government—1865–1950. 4. Reconstruction—South Carolina. I. Title.

F274.D7 1998

975.7'00496073—dc21 98-37819

CIP

TO HARRY AND ROSE CHOI

ACKNOWLEDGMENTS

My topic evolved out of research dealing with the impact of the Civil War and Reconstruction on children in South Carolina. The College of Charleston presented me with a sabbatical and a summer grant. Likewise, the Institute for Southern Studies at the University of South Carolina, Columbia, awarded me a summer research grant, which enabled ready access to the South Caroliniana Library and the South Carolina Department of Archives and History. My heartfelt thanks goes out to the staff at these three institutions. Linda Malone of the Fairfield County Museum in Winnsboro and Lowry Ware, an expert on Abbeville County, provided valuable material. I am grateful to Fred Bauman, manuscript librarian at the Manuscript Division of the Library of Congress. I would also like to thank Clarence Walker, William Hine, Paul Escott, and Winthrop Jordan for their insightful comments and critiques. But I owe a special debt of gratitude to Willard Gatewood for his support and help. Finally, my wife, Cheryle Drago, has been unstinting in her support.

CONTENTS

PREFACE

When the Civil War ended, the relationship between white and black Southerners was redefined, especially during Congressional Reconstruction, beginning in 1867. In most states of the former Confederacy, the term "Republican" became synonymous with "black." Except for "Aristocrats of Color," the role of black conservatives in the South has been minimized by both traditional and revisionist historians. The collective memory of Southerners, white and black, at least in South Carolina, seems to support this stance. However, the involvement of black Red Shirts in the campaign of 1876 to elect the Redeemer candidate, Wade Hampton, governor of South Carolina makes the story of Radical Reconstruction more complex. This study of ex-slaves who abetted a movement that led to white supremacy suggests that even today white conservatives may become more successful in wooing black voters.

Post-Revisionism

This study is post-revisionist. Since the 1970s historians have stressed the centrality of class during Reconstruction.[1] Still others have examined the role of gender. Perhaps the most serious criticism of revisionism has focused on its tendency toward romanticism. In a collection of hard-hitting and thoughtful essays, Clarence E. Walker counseled historians to "rise above the romantic and celebratory." Part of this challenge is to give serious attention to African Americans who did not fit the heroic-liberation mode, such as black Confederates and black Red Shirts.[2]

Community studies have not been free of romanticism either. As Walker suggested, for many American historians, especially scholars of black history, the term "community" has become "a romantic construct that obscures more than it reveals and posits community as unproblematic." Unity is stressed, often at the expense of diversity within the community. The resulting studies of black communities, in positing a vibrant black subculture, sometimes ignore or downplay their pathological aspects. Finally, by focusing too narrowly, scholars run the risk of making these black communities too autonomous. They skew the picture by failing to examine links to the larger communal setting.[3]

To understand the black Red Shirts, it is necessary to remember that black and white South Carolinians, especially in the Upcountry, seldom lived isolated from each other in racially exclusive communities. By practicing Protestantism, they shared some common cultural values that transcended race. By living in an overwhelmingly agrarian world, both blacks and whites nurtured a devotion to place and land. Having been mistreated, even abused, by Yankees, black South Carolinians also perceived Northerners as outsiders. Building on such distrust and other shared perceptions, Wade Hampton and his lieutenants were able to recruit black Red Shirts. Exactly how the dynamics played out at the local level will be suggested by focusing on Abbeville County as a test case.[4]

Reconstruction in South Carolina: A Summary

On June 30, 1865, President Andrew Johnson announced the conditions for restoring civil government in South Carolina. To implement his policy, he named prewar Unionist Benjamin F. Perry provisional governor. In September a constitutional convention was held. The Ordinance of Secession was nullified, slavery was abolished, and James L. Orr was nominated candidate for governor. Like Perry, he had opposed extremism. Orr barely defeated Wade Hampton, the former Confederate general, who had declined the nomination.

Presidential Reconstruction ended when Congress took over in 1867. With the advent of black suffrage, South Carolina remained in Republican hands between 1868 and 1876. White Republicans held the office of governor throughout the period: Robert Scott (1868–72), Franklin Moses Jr. (1872–74), and Daniel H. Chamberlain (1874–76). The legislature had a

Republican majority. More than half of the men elected to state and Federal offices during this period were blacks. Blacks even sat on the state supreme court. In 1870 they composed a majority of the legislature.

As early as the summer of 1865, the state's nearly four hundred thousand ex–slaves had begun adjusting to the new situation, including a different labor system. They regularized their marriages, organized their own churches, and participated in parades that celebrated freedom. Given the franchise during Congressional Reconstruction, the black population consolidated its gains. A middle class emerged, consisting of artisans, landowners, lawyers, doctors, clergymen, politicians, businessmen, and educators. They welcomed a public school system that would provide education for all South Carolinians, regardless of race.

The advent of a biracial Republican majority rule provoked a white backlash. White planters feared losing control over their workers. A number of black and white Republican leaders were assassinated. In 1869 the legislature responded by authorizing a state militia, composed largely of blacks. The specter of armed blacks, white South Carolina's worst nightmare, led to the state's branch of paramilitary organization, the Ku Klux Klan. With President Ulysses S. Grant's declaration of martial law in nine counties, nearly all in the Upcountry, the Klan was broken. Some of its leaders fled the state to avoid arrest and prosecution.

Congressional Reconstruction in South Carolina, weakened by economic recession, was further undermined by widespread corruption, which especially plagued the Republican administration under Franklin Moses, a South Carolinian. Attempts by reform Republicans and moderate Democrats to back independent candidates failed. The last Republican governor, Daniel Chamberlain, a New Englander, made real attempts to end corruption. Elected in 1874, he tried to hold together the party for one more gubernatorial election.

By 1876 the Republican Party in South Carolina was in disarray. An increasing number of black Republicans had grown disillusioned with a party that had become corrupt and unresponsive to their needs. In the summer of 1876, members of both parties attempted to field a fusionist ticket with Chamberlain heading it. When this failed, the state was turned into a political battleground, as Wade Hampton challenged Chamberlain for the governorship. For nearly all white South Carolinians, the issue was home rule. Hampton held out the possibility of peace with honor. In turn, many blacks, fed up with corruption, violence, and economic hard times, saw Hampton as representing the best of postwar paternalism. Throughout the state Hampton processions waved such slogans as "Peace and Prosperity to all Classes," "Honest and Good Government for All!" His campaign with its military paraphernalia became for many South Carolinians a crusade for redemption and reform.[5]

The election of 1876 was an especially important one. Nationally it decided who would sit in the White House: Republican Rutherford B. Hayes or Democrat Samuel J. Tilden. Hayes's election hinged on winning the electoral votes of several states such as South Carolina where the results were contested. A national bipartisan election committee supported Hayes, thereby insuring his victory. In the White House, Hayes ordered the withdrawal of the last troops from South Carolina.[6]

Organization of the Book

Hurrah for Hampton is among a rising genre that combines in-depth analysis with primary sources. It is divided into three chapters. "Wade Hampton's Black Red Shirts," the first chapter, proves that hundreds of ex-slaves, mostly from the Upcountry, participated in the Redemption campaign of 1876. Using a chart and a profile of twenty black Red Shirts (table 1), plus a voting table (table 2), this chapter examines these ex-slaves' mindset by placing them in the context of the times. Their war experiences as well as their slave experiences shaped their political responses as freedmen. Some, who had suffered from the war, resented Yankees as outsiders. They viewed Hampton as a real alternative to Republican corruption and continued violence. Their marching in Hampton processions blunted Republican charges that the Democrats were racists. In order to understand their significance, this study analyzed the role of women in the campaign. For their political beliefs, black Red Shirts endured physical and verbal abuse from black Republican women, who recognized that such men made a difference. Black Republican leaders and preachers encouraged the women. By attempting to stigmatize, even ostracize, the black Red Shirts, black

Republicans in general acknowledged that these men were indeed part of their community.

The second chapter, "South Carolina in 1876," contains the testimonies of seven black Red Shirts before a Congressional committee, composed of three United States senators who were investigating the election. These testimonies are arranged chronologically. They demonstrate how competent and forceful some of the black Red Shirt leaders were. The final chapter, "South Carolina Slave Narratives," includes the interviews, sixty years after the election, of ten black Red Shirts and the widow of an eleventh. It is organized alphabetically by their surnames. This chapter shows how the slave experience of some of the black Red Shirts predisposed them to join the Democrats. It proves that paternalism remained a powerful force that continued to shape the Southern experience.

The documents are an important part of the book, since they present in chorus a seldom-heard conservative voice. They offer the reader a glimpse into the motivations of black Red Shirts in their own words. To assist the reader, brief descriptions of the individuals are inserted in brackets at the beginning of their testimonies or narratives. Minor corrections and changes are also in brackets. These interviews offer the reader an opportunity to examine the relationship between black initiative and Southern paternalism.[7]

HURRAH FOR HAMPTON!

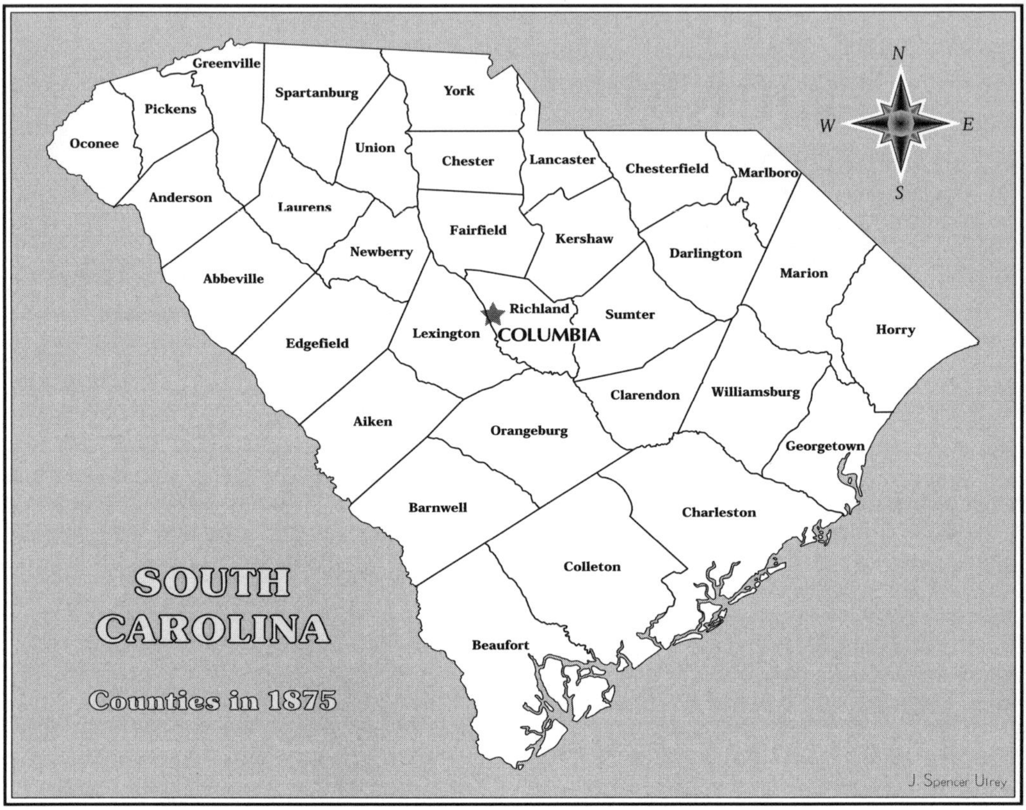
N
W
E
S
Greenville
Oconee
Pickens
Spartanburg
York
Union
Chester
Lancaster
Chesterfield
Marlboro
Anderson
Laurens
Fairfield
Kershaw
Darlington
Marion
Newberry
Abbeville
Richland
COLUMBIA
Sumter
Lexington
Edgefield
Horry
Clarendon
Williamsburg
Aiken
Orangeburg
Georgetown
Barnwell
Charleston
Colleton
Beaufort
SOUTH CAROLINA
Counties in 1875
J. Spencer Ulrey

WADE HAMPTON'S BLACK RED SHIRTS

> *The time Capt. Wade Hampton was stumping I followed him all over the State; I led 500 head; was with him to Camden, Orangeburg and all the way to Hampton County; led 500 negroes through the County; I was Captain of them; I rode 'Nellie Ponsa' and wore my red jacket and cap and boots; I had a sword too; my 'red shirt' died year before last.*
>
> —*Richard Mack, Black Red Shirt, Charleston County, 1937*

Introduction: A Forgotten Legacy

For posterity, Wade Hampton's supporters gathered for a group photograph, which was entitled *The True Patriots of the Age Standing by the Hero of 1876*. At the time most white South Carolinians perceived them as race heroes who had restored white supremacy in South Carolina. Ironically, as in so many other events in South Carolina history, the gathering was biracial. Standing on the far right of the former Confederate general was George M. Mears, a light-skinned black legislator from the Lowcountry. When Mears left the legislature in 1892, conservative whites gave him an engraved ebony cane with a gold head for his service to the cause. His Charleston descendants still hold onto it as a treasured keepsake of their heritage.[1]

Historians have demonstrated that some of Charleston's free brown elite joined with the Democrats. Hampton's black supporters also included Republicans like Martin R. Delany and ex-slaves such as Stephney Riley, a successful stable owner who was Charleston's most visible, if not most notorious, black Democrat. In September 1876 the white conservatives

Black legislator and Hampton supporter George Mears with his wife, Emma. *Avery Research Center for African American History and Culture, College of Charleston.*

requested Federal troops to protect their black allies. Shortly before Hampton's triumphal procession in the Holy City, black Democrats, led by Richard Holloway, met in prestigious Hibernian Hall, where most of them decided to march alongside the general. Hampton badges were made available for the participants.[2]

Republicans like Martin R. Delany were often perceived as mavericks by both contemporaries and historians. The Northern-born Delany appeared to have been motivated by a dislike of both brown and white Republicans. Charleston's free brown elite and entrepreneurs like Riley voted Democrat for political reasons but also to support their wealthy white patrons. However, what about those ex-slaves in the Upcountry who helped Wade Hampton redeem the state? Particularly those men who donned uniforms, often red shirts, and joined the Democrats in their processions and rallies? Rather than dismissing them as an aberration on the political landscape, it might be more fruitful to include them as another manifestation of black conservatism. Such black conservatives fit into a larger theme in African American history, namely a stream of blacks who have supported conservative regimes from the colonial period to the present. Yet most historians, traditional and revisionist, have given short shrift to the black Red Shirts and their role in what one historian has called a "counterrevolution."[3]

Traditional historians cite them only in passing. Recent historians, mostly revisionists, have tended to ignore these black Red Shirts or have downplayed their numbers and their "agency." This is understandable because it is hard to comprehend that freedmen would join a group or movement that terrorized Republicans. Moreover, the Democratic strategy of 1876 as outlined by Martin W. Gary advocated disinformation as well as intimidation and bribery against Republicans, white and black alike. Gary himself had little hope that blacks would willingly join the cause. Consequently, when Hampton Jarrell, a professor of English at Winthrop College, Rock Hill, wrote *Wade Hampton and the Negro,* he hardly mentioned the black Red Shirts. Joel Williamson, relying on Northern and Republican estimates, believed that the conservative press inflated their numbers. Williamson, a revisionist with Upcountry roots in Anderson County, argued that few blacks participated in the Democratic campaign. Relying on Williamson, Richard Zuczek conceded the existence of these black Red Shirts, but he concluded that they seemed more numerous than they were because the Democrats placed them conspicuously in processions and rallies. The only flesh-and-blood black Red Shirts Zuczek acknowledged are black Republicans intimidated into wearing the uniform.[4]

Vilified by other blacks, these supporters of General Hampton, many from the Upcountry, have disappeared from the collective memory of most black South Carolinians. One black Red Shirt, Andy Brice, recalled sixty years after Reconstruction ended in South Carolina: "I never was very popular wid my own color. They say behind my back, in '76, dat I's a white folks nigger."[5] The black Red Shirts have also remained faceless because Democrats sometimes withheld the names of black followers to protect them against Republican reprisals, especially by other blacks.[6] The rise to power of such racial demagogues as Benjamin R. Tillman and Coleman L. Blease insured that they would be forgotten. The result is that the black Red Shirt has remained relatively obscure or is depicted as either a victim or an opportunist.[7]

The compelling testimonies of seventeen black men suggest the need to re-evaluate the role of the black Red Shirt in the counterrevolution. Hundreds of Upcountry freedmen became Red Shirts. Most of them were dark-skinned and far less affluent than the Lowcountry black elite. While white Democrats were unwilling to allow them real authority within the party leadership, their support made a difference. Their participation in Hampton processions and rallies made it more difficult for South Carolina Republicans to prompt immediate Federal intervention. As their own words illustrate, some were leaders who were sincerely motivated, highly competent, and effective in winning black support for Hampton.

Taken collectively, the testimonies of these seventeen black men offer the reader a glimpse into the motivations and mind-set of the black Red Shirt. Seven testified to Congress on the election of 1876.[8] The other ten designated themselves as Red Shirts in the South Carolina slave narratives. One of these ten identified another black Red Shirt by name. A woman interviewed in these narratives described her dead husband as a black Red Shirt. Furthermore, in 1911 the *Columbia State* printed a photograph of a mounted black Red Shirt at a reunion. See the chart and table 1 for details about these twenty men.[9]

Like any source, these narratives and the Congressional testimonies pose problems. In both cases, the interviewers helped shape the responses. The seven blacks who identified themselves as Democrats at the Congressional hearings held in Columbia were cross-examined under oath by skeptical Republican committee members. The committee was composed of three U.S. senators with legal or judicial backgrounds. The chair was Angus

Cameron, a Republican lawyer from Wisconsin who had served in both houses of his state legislature. Michigan Senator Isaac P. Christiancy was a longtime Republican who had helped organize the party in 1854. From 1857 to 1875 he had sat on the Michigan State Supreme Court. The third member of the committee was Augustus Summerfield Merrimon, a Democrat from North Carolina, who had joined the Confederate army as a captain at the outbreak of the war. But in the fall of 1861 he had resigned to become solicitor for the eighth judicial district of his state during the war. Moreover, these black Red Shirts were acutely aware that their testimonies were to be taken under oath. When one of them was accosted by another black, the man responded, "No, I didn't come here to swear against my own color; I came here to swear the truth. Do you believe if am put on my oath I would swear a lie?"[10]

The slave narratives present thornier problems. Perhaps that is why recent historians, including Williamson and Zuczek, did not use them. These narratives were conducted nearly six decades after the end of Reconstruction, often by white interviewers with an Old South bias. Interviewed in their waning years during the Great Depression, some of the ex-slaves looked back romantically on those antebellum days when paternalistic masters took care of their elderly slaves. For them, the elections of 1876 and 1878 had blended into a collective Red Shirt experience. Therefore, they were unclear exactly when they were Red Shirts. Moreover, some saw their interview as an opportunity to obtain a government pension and responded accordingly. Black Red Shirt Ed Barber, for example, pleaded to the interviewer W. W. Dixon: "I begs you, in de name of de good white folks of '76 and Wade Hampton, not to forget me in dis old age pension business."[11]

William Woodward Dixon's background exemplifies the impact of the interviewer in shaping these narratives. Born in March 1868 at Woodward in Fairfield County, Dixon had close ties with some of the individuals he interviewed. As an infant, he had been nursed by Ellen, the first wife of Andy Brice. Another black Red Shirt, Frank Adamson, described going opossum hunting with the interviewer's father, Sam. W. W. Dixon was a graduate of The Citadel, Class of 1890. After a stint as commandant of the Virginia Military Prep School, he returned to Fairfield County to practice law at Winnsboro, and he served in the state legislature for one term, 1915–16. He wrote a history of Fairfield, which ran serially in the *Winnsboro*

Fairfield News and Herald. His command of local history and genealogy predisposed him to serve as a WPA interviewer in 1937.[12]

Interestingly, W. W. Dixon was distantly related to Thomas Dixon Jr., the author of *The Clansmen,* which had inspired D. W. Griffith's film *Birth of a Nation.* W. W. Dixon was forty-seven years old and a member of the South Carolina legislature when the movie made its debut. In 1937, during the interview of Nelson Cameron, Dixon boasted that Thomas Dixon had dedicated his book to Harriet Cameron, the "young mistress" of the ex-slave's father. According to Cameron, she had married Col. Leroy McAfee, who had come from North Carolina to organize the Ku Klux Klan in South Carolina. In both the movie and book, the hero's family name was Cameron. Actually, *The Clansmen* was dedicated to Colonel McAfee, whom the author described as his uncle and a Grand Titan of the Klan.[13] McAfee was the Grand Titan of Cleveland County in North Carolina. Various branches of the Klan in the Carolinas engaged in cooperative efforts.[14]

Dixon's interviews rescued the black Red Shirts from near oblivion. He interviewed the six black Red Shirts and the widow of another at a time when such men as Ellison "Cotton Ed" Smith and his supporters did not want to acknowledge any meaningful black contribution to Hampton's campaign. Dixon was able to get some of these ex-slaves to recall their participation in some detail because, as a child, he had been a Red Shirt himself. "Us both had red shirts," Ed Barber reminded him. "You was a ridin' a gray pony and I was aridin' a red mule." Dixon was eight years old at the time; Barber, sixteen. Both probably wore red shirts in the 1878 election.[15] In conducting these interviews, Dixon himself no doubt learned more about the role blacks had played in the Red Shirt movement.[16] His desire to interview black Red Shirts inflated their numbers in the slave narratives. But the phenomenon would have been documented regardless, because four additional black Red Shirts were interviewed by others. Richard Mack, a black Red Shirt leader, was interviewed in Charleston by Martha S. Pinckney. He was the most enthusiastic in explaining his role in the election of 1876. Recalling many years later their involvement in Wade Hampton's campaign, both Dixon and Mack wanted the black Red Shirt phenomenon to be recorded. It still remained a graphic part of their historical memory.[17]

Prelude to the November 1876 Election: The Hamburg Riot and the Gary Plan

In early May 1876 it appeared that Republican governor Daniel H. Chamberlain would easily win re-election. Blacks held a voting majority of some twenty to thirty thousand votes. Moreover, while Chamberlain had overcome opposition within his party, the Democrats were split between fusionists (cooperationists) and straightouters. The editor of the *Charleston News and Courier,* Francis W. Dawson, and other fusionists recommended that their party concede the governorship to Chamberlain but put up candidates for the other offices. The straightouters, on the other hand, wanted to contest all the offices.[18]

Any chance of cooperation with Chamberlain ended with the Hamburg riot of July 1876. On the Fourth of July, two whites returning to their home in Edgefield passed through Hamburg (located in Aiken County but formerly part of Edgefield County). Apparently, they were jostled by a local black militia company drilling in the street. The father of one of the men obtained a warrant for the leader of the black militia, Doc Adams. At the trial the black magistrate, Prince Rivers, had Adams arrested for contempt of court. The trial was to be continued on July 8 with Edgefield lawyer Matthew C. Butler, a staunch straightouter, acting as prosecutor. The former Confederate general, with the support of some two to three hundred armed whites, demanded that the black militia surrender its arms. Adams steadfastly refused. Rivers tried to mediate, but both sides refused to back down. The black militia members took up a position in their armory, a brick building; shots were fired. After twenty-five to twenty-nine blacks were captured and rounded up, four were singled out and murdered. According to Republican and Democratic accounts, at least one white and seven blacks, including a marshal and a lieutenant of the militia, were killed.[19]

Although the conservative press generally condemned the lawlessness of the whites in killing these unarmed blacks, the Hamburg affair ultimately led to a polarization of the two parties and the end of fusionism. Most Republicans felt that the riot was the beginning of a campaign of violence, modeled after the Mississippi plan (later known as the Edgefield or

Shotgun policy). Butler, who was a leader of the Edgefield County rifle clubs, was arraigned as a participant in the riot. His close association with the author of the Shotgun policy, Martin W. Gary, only confirmed Republican suspicions. White Democrats, on the other hand, saw the riot as a logical outgrowth of arming a black militia. Their worst fears were aroused. With his chances of winning the gubernatorial nomination on the wane, Butler wisely withdrew and nominated Wade Hampton, another straightouter, who had a more moderate reputation—a reputation that could appeal to fusionists and perhaps even blacks.[20]

Most Democratic Party leaders realized that to defeat Republican governor Chamberlain on November 7, they had to come to grips with the black majority. "Unless the people get a portion of the colored voters to go with them," a Greenville newspaper predicted, "there can be no redemption of the State." After Wade Hampton secured the Democratic Party's gubernatorial nomination in August 1876, the newspaper asserted: "Every one of them who is induced to vote for Hampton reduces the formidable Republican majority, and adds one to the cause of redemption. Thus it acts with double force."[21]

A dual strategy evolved. Wade Hampton took the high road, wooing black voters with a pledge to protect their hard-won rights. His chief lieutenant, Martin Gary, followed the low road, the so-called Edgefield or Shotgun policy, which had proved so effective in redeeming Mississippi in 1875. While Hampton had a genuine paternalistic regard for blacks, while Gary had a real disgust for them, the difference between the two men was probably not so clear-cut. Hampton needed Gary and the threat of force he wielded, while Gary needed the kinder and gentler Hampton, whose appeal might make inroads into the black Republican majority and forestall Federal intervention.[22]

The Democratic campaign took on the organization of a military operation, and Gary's "Plan of the Campaign of 1876" read like a battle strategy. General Hampton's chief advisers were former Confederate generals, including M. C. Butler and Martin Gary. Other generals, like Johnson Hagood in Barnwell, Samuel P. McGowan in Abbeville, and John Bratton in Fairfield, were responsible for organizing Democrats in their own counties. In 1937, Louisa Davis recalled how her husband, a former slave, was "a red shirt long side General Bratton in '76."[23] Gen. James Connor was in charge of the state's rifle and sabre clubs, often led by ex-Confederate officers. These local groups provided the Democrats with a paramilitary force, their answer to the predominantly black state militia.[24] By 1876 Connor commanded some 290 clubs across the state with roughly 14,350 members.[25]

Given the military nature of the clubs, it was logical that uniforms would evolve. One historian noted that the troops of South Carolina Confederate regiments marched once again in arms, this time wearing red shirts instead of gray uniforms. In reality, Hampton's followers wore a variety of outfits in different colors, and not all the mounted men rode on horses. Describing a Democratic rally held at Williamston in Anderson County at the end of September 1876, an Upcountry newspaper reporter claimed: "The mounted men on horses and mules numbered near 2,000. Twenty odd clubs were represented. Blue jackets, red jackets, grey jackets, green jackets, and some without jackets."[26] However, as the movement gained momentum, the red shirt became the symbol of a Confederate nationalism which blossomed during the campaign of 1876.[27]

The actual origin of the red shirts is a bit murky. According to Alfred Williams, they first appeared as a uniform after the Hamburg riot in early September 1876. Indicted for murder, members of the Sweetwater Sabre Club, who had come to the town of Aiken for an arraignment, wore homespun shirts painted red. The shirts were a response to the bravado of the U.S. senator from Indiana, Oliver P. Morton, who waved a bloody shirt to rally the North behind Radical Reconstruction.[28] The Republican press thought "the new democratic uniform of a 'blood besprinkled shirt'. . . very appropriate, especially for the Aiken club, which distinguished itself at Hamburg." Shortly the men were simply called "Bloody Shirts."[29] Most accounts deny any connection with Garibaldi's Red Shirts, but the Italian nationalist appealed to the romanticism of white Southerners. His campaign to unify Italy began in 1860. That year, shortly before his election as governor of South Carolina, Francis W. Pickens evoked the name of Garibaldi to justify the secession movement as a fight against tyranny. In his "Reminiscences of the Confederate War," John Cheves Haskell commemorated fellow officer Bradfute Warren of Richmond, who had joined Garibaldi and served as a major in the Italian army, only to die on a battlefield in Virginia. Not surprisingly, many South Carolinians in the Hampton

Legion wore red shirts as part of their uniform during the war, while the women proudly wore Garibaldi hats.[30]

Gary's plan mandated that club members wear red shirts at all public gatherings, especially on election day. Gary was intent on using them to create an impressive spectacle.[31] Between August and November 1876 women eagerly went to work supporting their men much as they had during the war. Red flannel shirts appeared everywhere as South Carolina women produced tens of thousands of them.[32] According to one traditional historian, these women also fed every hungry Democrat who passed by their homes, which sometimes included a whole company of Red Shirts.[33] It became the fashion for women to wear red ribbons around their waists or in their hair.[34]

Wearing a red shirt became a rite of passage for young males who had been children during the war. They welcomed the opportunity to join their fathers and older brothers, who were veterans, in a campaign to redeem their state. Particularly in rural areas, these boys flocked to rallies in their red shirts, determined to assert their manhood by shouting as loud as the veterans. The *Newberry Herald* noted with relish that "the Town boys were also in the saddle, conspicuous in their red jackets." The veterans found themselves restraining their unruly and sometimes reckless young recruits. Even those too young to carry guns or to vote were recruited, for they could still swell the long processions in their red shirts.[35]

The Red Shirt procession ending in a rally evolved into a political ritual that was finely honed by the middle of September. Wherever Hampton went, thousands marched with him in these paramilitary parades. Such events thrilled the party faithful, made the cause seem invincible, struck fear in the hearts of Republican opponents, and blurred class differences among whites.[36] Various Upcountry towns vied to outdo one another, but by mid-September "the most sensational meeting of the campaign thus far was at Abbeville." The women had worked feverishly to prepare for the rally. They had made flags, sewed uniforms, decorated the speakers' stand, and encouraged their children to attend. According to a local account, they "did everything but 'jine the cavalry.'" On Friday, September 15, Hampton was greeted at the railroad depot by a band playing "Red, White and Blue." He stayed at "Mrs. Norwood's splendid mansion." That night the town

White Red Shirt Thomas Jefferson Lyon. *South Carolina Confederate Relic Room and Museum, Columbia.*

was "ablaze" with an impressive torchlight parade. On Saturday morning, when the marshal-in-charge gave the marching order, clubs from the counties of Anderson, Edgefield, Newberry, and Laurens joined the Abbeville clubs. Thirty-five hundred mounted men and fifteen hundred on foot marched in a procession that stretched some three miles long. Men, women, children, and elderly citizens lined Main Street to get a glimpse of them. The speeches opened with a prayer. Col. James S. Cothran, the county Democratic chairman, introduced Wade Hampton to an audience in the thousands, which included a number of blacks. Few could keep away from such a spectacle.[37]

Organizing the Black Vote: Gary's Plan Modified

Gary's "Plan of 1876" outlined prescriptions for handling and organizing blacks. The strategy required every Democrat to control at least one black vote, by intimidation or bribery. Several specific groups were targeted: property owners who paid taxes; those held in esteem by whites; the poorest blacks, who were dependent on whites; and, finally, those of weak character. Gary called for whites to organize sympathetic blacks into Democratic clubs beginning in September; if organizing failed, clubs were to be prefabricated. He obviously doubted that many such clubs would be established.[38] Consequently, Gary desired to implement in toto the Mississippi Plan of 1875. However, given South Carolina's vigorous black leadership and the presence of a black militia, an unrestrained approach could have backfired, fueling Republican calls for greater Federal intervention. Realizing this, Hampton modified Gary's hard-line strategy. Furthermore, as a genuine paternalist, Hampton wanted to woo the black vote. After the Hamburg riot, he subtly distanced himself from both Hamburg and Edgefield County. On August 9, the Republican *Columbia Daily Union-Herald* reported: "The Edgefield democrats are being badly snubbed. Neither Hampton nor [Gen. Joseph B.] Kershaw accepted the invitation to speak there yesterday."[39] Likewise, the Democratic Party openly disassociated itself from some of Gary's tactics that could lead to more Federal troops being brought into the state.

Undaunted, Gary and his straightouters interrupted Republican meetings, demanding equal time. They simply wanted to intimidate black voters and their leaders. Chamberlain publicly denounced such harassment in response to an invitation by A. C. Haskell, chair of the Democratic State Executive Committee, to attend Democratic meetings across the state. Haskell, in turn, sent out directives telling Democrats that division of time was to be used to appeal to black voters, not to terrorize them.[40]

Some white Democratic clubs (including the Red Shirts) admitted blacks into their ranks. The Florence Red Shirt Mounted Club, located in the Pee Dee region, had two black members.[41] Black and white members of the Dover, Fairfield, Lexington, and Congaree clubs rode together in the Hampton procession held in the state capital shortly before the election.[42] Pen Eubanks of Union County joined the Fairforest Red Shirt club, named after a white Baptist church. He and other black members summoned whites to the church, which became the club's meeting place. Eubanks eventually became the flag bearer for the unit, a position of honor.[43]

The Democrats were most successful in organizing large black clubs in predominantly black counties where the efforts were headed by former Confederate generals who shared Hampton's paternalistic attitude. Barnwell County is an example, illustrating how the dual Democratic strategy worked. The sheer violence advocated by Gary and his associates was complemented by the paternalistic efforts of Hampton and his followers to get the black vote. As chair of the Democratic campaign in this county, Johnson Hagood had his work cut out for him. Barnwell had a Republican majority of eighteen hundred, nearly all blacks. But the county had blacks willing to aid the general. One former slave, Sandy N. Sanders, had been considering organizing a conservative club since the beginning of Radical Reconstruction. The black farmer, who had known Hagood for forty years, suggested to his neighbors on Port Royal Road that they establish a club. He became president of a club with nearly one hundred members. Hagood supported Sanders's efforts by attempting to reduce violence against the blacks, which had become rampant in Barnwell. Hagood even suggested that Wade Hampton would quit if the rifle clubs initiated any more violence. By November 2, there were eighteen Democratic black clubs with a total of 668 members. Some black landholders backed Hagood, but preferred not to be officially enrolled in the clubs.[44]

Blacks participated in the Hampton campaign in a variety of ways.

Some simply marched on foot in the processions. Others were mounted, sometimes in separate "colored" Tilden-Hendricks Democratic clubs. Like their white counterparts, they appeared in uniforms of different colors, including yellow and blue. Most, however, wore the red shirt. Ex-slave Cureton Milling of Winnsboro disdainfully recalled that the red shirt had a special appeal. "Had they a black shirt I don't believe niggers would ever have took to it," he concluded. "They is too black already to suit de most of them." For young men, barely out of their teens, it was pretty heady stuff to don the red shirt and join thousands of Confederate veterans in a mile-long procession. For some, it marked their entry into manhood. Charley Barber could not wait to be given a red shirt by whites. The twenty-year-old man bought one with his first wages as a section hand on the railroad.[45]

These black men, demonstrating their skills as horsemen alongside Confederate veterans, manifested the prestige they felt. In commenting on the black cavalrymen who "rode side by side with their white friends," a reporter at a Sumter meeting noted: "The colored riders took great pride in their flashy red outfits, and were to be seen dashing in every direction on swift horses or stimulated mules, for the purposes of order and display."[46] The slave narratives captured the pride and élan of these black Red Shirts. Sixty years later, the details were still vivid. "Sho was a pretty sight to see 'bout a hun'ded mens up on fine horses wid red shirts on. I still sees dem in my mind clear as day," Pen Eubanks remembered nostalgically. "Our red shirts fastened wid a strong band 'round de waist. Dar wasn't nar'y speck o' white to be seed no whars on 'em."[47] These men were made to feel that they were an important part of the cause. At a Due West rally, "four hundred uniformed colored Democrats" dined "at tables prepared in the basement rooms of the college building [probably Erskine]."[48] According to Frank Adamson, "a nice white lady" in Columbia was so taken by his cheering loudly for Hampton, that she patted the Red Shirt on the shoulder and handed him two biscuits and a chicken drumstick. The woman thanked God for black men like Adamson.[49]

The most prestigious black Red Shirts may have formed a mounted black cadre comprising about five hundred members that accompanied Hampton across the state. They followed the general everywhere, including Beaufort and other coastal counties where white Democrats had difficulty in recruiting sizable numbers of mounted blacks. Richard Mack and other blacks who had served in the war with their masters probably formed the cadre. Mack claimed he headed a five-hundred-man black unit that traveled with Hampton "all over the State."[50] Joseph O'Bannon, a black Red Shirt from Barnwell County, recalled accompanying the Hampton cavalcade through this Midlands county in 1876. However, he refused to ride with the main body of "raw recruits" because he had "military training." In 1861, he had gone to the front with the three Hagood brothers, Augustus, Thomas, and William.[51] Many years after Reconstruction ended in South Carolina, both men still gloried in the roles they had played in the redemption of the state.

Older men, such as O'Bannon and Mack, who had learned their military skills as body servants to their masters during the Civil War, were ideal candidates to become Red Shirts. The wartime experience fostered a bond between their masters and them. The Red Shirt campaign offered them a chance to be part of the last crusade. O'Bannon had earned admiration for his skill in foraging, and when Augustus Hagood was wounded during the war, O'Bannon brought him home to the Hagood family.[52] Richard Mack had accompanied his master Captain Cherry and two other Confederate captains. They endured together the hardships, including eating hardtack and carrying the dead and wounded off the battlefield. The shared experience resulted in a kind of male bonding. Cherry asked Mack: "Why weren't you white!" When Cherry died, Mack became an orderly for Gen. Frank Bamberg and his brother Isaac. By doing odd jobs, Mack accumulated thousands of dollars in Confederate currency by the end of the war. "If we had won," he laughed, "I would be rich."[53]

Mack and O'Bannon were part of a long line of ex-slaves who accompanied white South Carolinians in nearly all the American wars of the nineteenth century. William Rose's life personifies such service. Born in Charleston in 1813, Rose came to Columbia when he was twelve years old. He was a drummer with the Richland Volunteers during the war with the Seminoles. In the Mexican War he served as a body servant with the Palmetto Regiment. When the Civil War broke out, he became the valet for Gen. Maxcy Gregg.[54] In 1923, South Carolina officially recognized blacks' contributions to the Confederacy by passing a statute that gave pensions to blacks who had served at least six months. Faced with a flood of applications, the state amended the act in 1924 by disallowing "all laborers, teamsters, and non-South Carolinians." Only "body-servants or male camp cooks" were eligible. Roughly 287 received pensions.[55]

Black musicians were also likely Red Shirt recruits. Some had served in the Confederacy as musicians.[56] During the campaign of 1876, they provided entertainment at Hampton's rallies, creating a festive atmosphere. Andy Brice played his fiddle at dances for whites. He told W. W. Dixon: "I wear a red shirt then, drink red liquor, play de fiddle at de 'lection box, and vote de white folks ticket."[57] Black brass bands played a prominent role in the parades and processions that highlighted the campaign. Black bands performing at Hampton events included the Newberry Brass Band, the Abbeville "Colored" Brass Band, the Wilmington "Colored" Brass Band, and the Columbia "Colored" Brass Band.[58] Although the Democrats hired or funded these black bands, some were supported by blacks themselves. When the Winnsboro brass band wanted to play at a Hampton rally in Camden, Ouillah Harrison, using his four-horse team, transported the group at his own expense. Naming his newborn son after Wade Hampton, the black teamster later told the boy to remember his namesake and to "always vote a straight out democrat ticket."[59]

The Hampton Strategy: Solidify the Upcountry Base

Hampton's campaign concentrated first on the Upcountry, where he was sure of solid support. Then he went to the Midlands, saving the Lowcountry, with its large black majority, for last. As Hampton campaigned southward, he experienced success. His cavalcade was joined by other black and white club members at various rally sites across the state.[60] Their numbers at these political rallies were further increased by young men looking for a quick handout. Ed Barber of Winnsboro acknowledged that if a black man was hungry, all he had to do was to "go to de white folk's house, beg for a red shirt," and say he was a Democrat. If he did not get a red shirt the first time around, he at least got "his belly full of everything de white folks got" and the "privilege" of coming back to the "trough."[61] Hampton's targeting of the Upcountry was politically wise. By mid-September Republican newspapers conceded a dramatic increase in the Democratic vote in the "up-country, north of the north line of Richland county."[62]

The Lower Piedmont counties of the Upcountry were more problematic. Since 1850 the planting of cotton, a one-crop economy, had spread into the Lower Piedmont. That year the region produced 138,896 bales of cotton while the Upper Piedmont recorded 35,797. With cotton came an increase in the slave population. More than half the population of the Lower Piedmont was black.[63] Concurrently, more whites became involved in the cotton economy and plantation slavery. By the 1850s even the yeoman farmers, once relatively independent, found themselves tied to growing cotton. In 1868, these counties became hotbeds of Ku Klux Klan activity because whites used intimidation to carry elections in a region so evenly divided racially between whites and blacks.[64] Consequently, the Lower Piedmont region posed a conundrum to the Democrats in 1876. To build a successful majority, they had to appeal to blacks while not alienating whites, especially yeoman farmers. In Abbeville County, for example, black voters outnumbered white voters by 4,951 to 2,928 in 1875. The Republicans had carried this county by nearly 1,500 votes in 1874.[65] Complicating the Democratic Party's task was the success Republicans had experienced in wooing whites disillusioned by the war and undergoing economic hard times. The Democratic campaign in Abbeville County illustrated how the Redeemers overcame this problem.

Abbeville County: A Case Study

After the war, many blacks and whites found themselves in poverty. When an Abbeville black Republican was asked if "the poor white men work much" in the county, he answered: "Yes, sir; the poor white men and the colored works nobly." Although he further explained that the poor whites were "a heap harder on the colored people than the other white men," a local Democratic newspaper in July 1876 feared that poor whites and poor blacks had the potential of keeping Abbeville Republican. "The negroes and poor whites," the Abbeville *Medium* noted, "took charge of the ga-lorious Fourth in these parts last week and tried to get up an excitement."[66] With so many whites alienated by the war, the *Medium* opposed the straightout ticket when Gen. M. C. Butler headed it because there were "too many military characters for peaceable men. Some of these men will do, but ninety-nine out of every hundred men in the State would not vote for the ticket."[67] Fortunately for the Democrats, Butler withdrew to support Hampton.

The Democrats in Abbeville County were also fortunate in that the local Republican leaders were divided—so much so that they were demoralized and ineffective as the redemption movement gained momentum. In August 1876, a member of the Republican County executive committee asked Governor Chamberlain, "I wish to know whether I am right in my understanding or not whereas there being so many of our men fighting you in this county." The man added that, while he intended to support the governor as he had in 1874, he wanted something for his efforts.[68] By mid-September a Greenville Republican noted that the Upcountry Republicans were demoralized, especially in Abbeville and Anderson, "owing in part to Hampton's raid [campaign], and in part to certain names on our ticket."[69] A few days before the November election, Abbeville Republican Benjamin F. Moore wrote to the governor: "The Republican leaders dont take hold of the cause like they should, (you can see yourself, from the nos. of Col. men that have joined the Democratic ranks)."[70]

Honest government was a serious issue all over the state. Even revisionists have conceded that after 1869 Republicans engaged in fraud and corruption that justified some of the most vicious charges made by conservatives against them.[71] Corruption and mismanagement were a central concern particularly in the Upcountry. A Newberry Democrat friendly to Chamberlain informed the governor, "Peace, order, and good government" were all that the plain farmers wanted, "regardless of party."[72] In his letter to Chamberlain, Abbeville Republican Benjamin Moore blamed the conservative press for creating such issues as corruption and mismanagement. At the same time, Moore promised to deliver Calhoun's Mill precinct and the entire county if he were given 150 to 200 dollars. "I can with this aid from you," he pleaded, "bribe the majority if not all the Col. Democrats." He continued, "I have promised to pay them something if they would meet me on my plantation and go with me to the polls. . . . I don't think we can achieve a victory any other way but by paying them."[73]

By contrast, the Redeemers in Abbeville County were led by such respected and capable men as Gen. Samuel McGowan and Col. James S. Cothran, who were not uncompromising. When it was suggested that McGowan be nominated for governor, a leading Columbia Republican newspaper commented: "Sam is too good a man to be slaughtered that way."[74] In early May, Cothran supported a fusionist ticket with Chamberlain at its head.[75] As the Democratic chairman of Abbeville County, Cothran was willing to reach out to blacks, who made up more than 60 percent of its eligible voters in 1875.[76] Furthermore, the efforts of McGowan and Cothran were supported by Robert R. Hemphill, co-editor of the *Abbeville Medium*. The paper was effective in offsetting the hard-line policy of the Democratic *Abbeville Press and Banner.*

However, in May, shortly after Cothran and other fusionists had opposed Gary, an elderly white couple, John and Catherine Harmon of Abbeville County, were found murdered. Six blacks who were convicted of the crime were peremptorily shot to death by a mob.[77] The Hamburg riot in July made it even more difficult for the Democrats to appeal to blacks. On July 19, the *Medium* recognized that some local blacks were upset about the riot and its repercussions.[78]

By the end of July, the incendiary Hamburg "fever" had spread to the town of Abbeville. The *Press and Banner* claimed that "four or five thousand negroes" came to the town on Friday, July 28. It described "armed bodies of negroes roaming about the streets, discharging their rifles." Another Democratic newspaper called upon "Governor Chamberlain to bring the Abbeville negro rioters to justice." Actually most of the blacks had come to see the public hanging of a black man. The Republicans used the opportunity to hold a caucus. The Abbeville County sheriff reported that the blacks were "orderly and unarmed," but that a "a row was imminent" because of "an armed mob of twenty five or thirty men from Edgefield which caused all the excitement. They came to Abbeville to make a row, and were only prevented by the interference of some of our best citizens," who urged peace. A Republican newspaper blamed the Harmon affair and the Hamburg riot for poisoning race relations in the town, creating an atmosphere of "distrust and antagonism instead of confidence and mutual good will. This is of recent growth in Abbeville."[79] The paper congratulated "the order-loving citizens of Abbeville" for demanding "that the

Edgefield Sioux shall keep on their reservations."[80] Northern newspapers referred to Butler and his Edgefield contingent as "Sitting Bull Butler and his Hamburg Sioux."[81]

In mid-October, the Abbeville Democrats and Republicans decided to hold separate rallies on the same day. While the Democrats met at the courthouse, the Republicans gathered at the "colored fairground." The Democratic leaders took every measure possible to keep their men in order. They tactfully declined the offer of the Edgefield and Laurens clubs to march at their rally. A Republican newspaper commented: "The conduct of the Abbeville democratic leaders is in marked contrast with those of Newberry. One reason of it may be that the people respect such men as [Samuel] McGowan, and therefore obey them."[82]

To win black support, Cothran and other conservatives made a plausible case, combining carrot and stick. Lewis Clay, a black Republican running for county commissioner of Abbeville, recalled the arguments Democrats used: "The republican party was rogues, and was stealing, and if we was to vote for them we would be ruining ourselves as well as them, and that we couldn't get no lands to live upon." Clay continued: "They . . . wouldn't allow us to live on their land if we voted the Republican ticket; but that, if we voted with them, we would have good homes and good government, and be taken care of . . . and they promised a heap of them that if they voted with them they would let them live on their place for low rent."[83]

Actually, the conservative campaign was more sophisticated than Clay realized. With most of the wealth and education of the county on their side, the Democrats were able to confer "respectability" on right-thinking blacks. In August, the *Abbeville Medium* lauded twenty-three "Colored Democrats" as "the best men of their color—honest, industrious, good citizens who have amassed considerable property and have an interest in good government."[84] The weekly told blacks in September, "Their safest place in this campaign and for all time to come is on the side of virtue, honesty and intelligence, among the white people," who would "guarantee all the rights of the colored man under the constitution and ask them to help in purifying the government and saving the State."[85] When black Republicans informed black Democrat Edward Henderson that "his politics were obnoxious to the colored people about town" and that he should leave, the

Medium defended him as "a respectable colored man, who has succeeded in getting fifty-four members to the colored Tilden and Hendricks club."[86] The newspaper praised Henderson and other black Democrats as "noble, manly and gallant" for their support in the campaign.[87]

The Democrats had recruited enough blacks to win the Abbeville municipal election held September 11. The *Medium* gloated: "The colored people . . . voted the 'straight-out' ticket in open defiance of all their pledges to the Republican party."[88] According to one conservative account, the election of W. H. Parker, "one of the most distinguished and venerated citizens of upper Carolina," as town intendant or mayor particularly "gave Abbeville people a taste of good old times."[89] After the victory, the town council appointed two marshals, including a black one, to show "that the Democrats are willing to divide the honors and emoluments of office with the colored people."[90] Even *Cincinnati Commercial* reporter H. V. Redfield, described as "a bitter partisan Radical Republican" by a conservative journalist, had to admit the Democrats were making inroads. Witnessing the results of this local election, Redfield reversed his earlier prediction that Chamberlain would easily win re-election. "Abbeville has heretofore been undeniably Republican," he noted. "The whites hardly thought of carrying it until this campaign, for the blacks outnumber the whites more than two to one." Out of the 276 votes cast, blacks accounted for 143, of which 100 went Democrat. An additional 263 blacks failed to vote. Proclaiming the Abbeville results as "a very large straw," Redfield concluded that the Democrats would win decidedly if they could "apply the same rule to the whole state."[91] Colonel Cothran himself was successfully recruiting blacks. In Due West, "a splendid supper was given to the colored Democrats . . . by the gentlemen of the village." After a "spirited speech" by Cothran, "a large number of recruits were received into the Democratic ranks."[92]

Abbeville Democrats described their policy toward blacks as "The Preference Policy."[93] John Crawford, a black Democratic barber in Abbeville, received more business than he could handle—"a perfect windfall."[94] As Republicans were quick to point out, the preference policy had its prescriptive side. Theoretically, those who did not vote Democratic would not be hired, or those who voted Republican could be turned off the land. In practice, however, some planters only gave lip service to the policy. When planting time came, they hired every hand they could get. "Many of the most pronounced Radical negroes in this place," complained the *Abbeville Medium,* "openly boast that they receive plenty of work from the Democrats and that, if anything, they get more work to do now and better pay than they did before preference or prescription was mentioned or thought of."[95]

Some black Democrats in Abbeville County belonged to rifle clubs. "The Hampton Tigers," the rifle club from Bordeaux, numbered forty whites and forty-five blacks. It was under the leadership of W. H. Peake. The most effective of these white recruiters was Thomas Young, a thirty-four-year-old miller, originally from North Carolina. He founded a "Tilden and Hendricks colored club" in Lowndesville. Young had never been a Democratic Party regular or a particularly partisan Democrat. In fact, in 1874 he voted for Chamberlain, the "best" person. However, in 1876 he supported a "right honest democratic ticket." Hampton appealed to him. "I knew him when [I] was a boy and ran with him in the mountains sometimes," the recruiter explained. "I had a friendly feeling toward him, as being straightforward and honest man, and a man who would do justice to the colored man as well as the white man."[96] Young's black group may have been one of the thirteen rifle clubs listed for Abbeville County. The men wore "yellow shirts, trimmed with black braid, black pants and patent leather caps." According to a local newspaper, "they ride good stock and do some splendid shouting." The black unit carried a flag presented by "Miss Eliza Tusten, of this place."[97]

Young was successful because he was able to work with blacks such as Tom Lomax, a twenty-five-year-old black farmer who had spoken at Republican meetings. When Lomax became a Democrat, Young recognized his abilities. In Young's absence, Lomax led the mounted Lowndesville contingent.[98] Democratic victory depended on this ability to attract and work with capable black leaders, who could articulate the hardships blacks were undergoing. In August, Thomas Burgess, a black Baptist, began organizing a black Democratic club in Cokesbury. The following month the *Abbeville Medium* printed his letter entitled "To my Race." Burgess, a resident of Hodges, Abbeville County, ridiculed carpetbaggers as "rogues" who "fooled us by their false promises, such as the 'forty acres and a mule.'" Burgess continued, "If anybody will get a mule it will be me; but it will not come from these scalawags."[99] Such logic appealed to Asbury Green and other Abbeville County blacks, who were disillusioned with Republican rule. Green joined some twenty other blacks in a Hodges Depot Democratic club. A slave before the war, he scraped by as a sharecropper, barely supporting his wife and five children. No matter how hard he worked, things seemed to get worse under the Republicans. He felt swindled by them. "I can't support my family," he explained, "I want a change in the government." The Democrats gave him money, a Red Shirt, and a horse to ride.[100]

The three most influential black Democrats in Abbeville County were Richard Roman, Aaron Mitchell, and Edward Henderson. Richard Roman, a resident of Abbeville township, was a twenty-five-year-old farmer who practiced the preference policy, employing fifteen black Democrats to pick cotton on his farm. Roman took the charges of Republican corruption seriously. The speeches of Chamberlain, Cothran, and McGowan convinced him that the Republicans had levied high taxes, squandered the money, and concomitantly defrauded the state. At the Congressional hearings, Roman cited specific cases of Republican corruption, particularly a Solomon's Bank scandal.[101]

Roman, a tireless campaigner who traveled throughout the county, was a particularly effective stump speaker. At the end of September, he spoke along with McGowan and Cothran at an important Lowndesville rally. There was an "unusually large attendance of colored people." The procession of "1,000 mounted men" included Thomas Young's black club of 117.[102] Although the *Abbeville Medium* credited Young with most effectively delivering the black vote in the county, Roman boasted: "I advised a heap of them to join with me myself. I did more about organizing that two hundred and eighty men than any white man in the county."[103]

"Big Aaron" was a sixty-year-old blacksmith-mechanic who worked mostly for whites. He had eight shops, which required him to travel some thirty-two miles coming and going between them and his home in Abbeville. Mitchell had originally been a Republican and had served briefly as town marshal. But he grew more disillusioned over local Republican politics, which was dominated by the Guffin brothers, Lemuel, Lawrence, and Charles. In 1871, Lemuel was a probate judge; Lawrence was a legislator; and Charles was the intendant, or mayor, of Abbeville. That year

Mitchell was relieved from duty as town marshal and replaced by another black Republican. The Guffin family, "which had lived in the area for a century," had a stranglehold over the black voters. According to Lemuel Guffin's obituary, "his power in controlling his followers and his ability for quieting opposition, was notable."[104]

After studying the political situation for years, Aaron Mitchell decided to switch to the Democrats. In August 1876, he approached General McGowan, who asked, "Is that possible?" Mitchell replied, "Yes." The blacksmith stumped all over the county for the Democratic ticket, attending some thirteen meetings. By conservative accounts, he was very successful. Although illiterate, he obviously had a sense of command.[105] At a Hampton rally in the town of Abbeville, "the handsomest transparency in the line was that of THE MEDIUM, carried by that Vulcan of the Colored Democracy, Aaron Mitchell."[106] In late September, the Abbeville paper reported: "Aaron Mitchell, 'big Aaron,' is doing good work among the colored people. On Saturday he succeeded in gaining eleven colored recruits to the Democratic ranks. He proposes to stump the county for the reform ticket."[107] At Due West, before an audience of "four hundred uniformed colored Democrats," Mitchell gave an after-dinner speech that was "especially good and had a very happy effect on the large crowd of colored people present."[108] About two weeks before the election, he gave a similar speech at Antreville. According to the *Medium,* "[I]t had a good effect as was plainly discernible from the countenances of the audience who gave him their undivided attention."[109] When testifying before the Congressional committee on the 1876 elections, Mitchell never got rattled. Although he had been appointed town marshal for a while, he apparently had never run for an elected office. Asked what offices he had held, he replied, "Nothing, sir, but a hammer in my hand and an anvil."[110]

Perhaps the most important president of a black Democratic club in Abbeville County was an ex-slave, Edward Henderson, a forty-eight-year-old carpenter. A Democrat since 1867, Henderson worked well with Cothran. Despite intimidation, he had recruited at least fifty-four black members into the Abbeville club by early September. In part because of his efforts, the Democrats were able to carry the September municipal election in Abbeville, a watershed in their campaign. Two days after the election, Cothran declared: *"Let every colored Democrat have a place in the mounted procession.*" Henderson captained a mounted club whose members wore blue shirts. One hundred and eight strong, they marched in the grand Democratic rally held in mid-September at Abbeville. On September 20, the *Abbeville Medium* reported that "Captain Edward Henderson gave a most sumptuous dinner to the members of the Tilden and Hendricks Club of this place and the colored gentlemen of other clubs who were in town last Saturday to welcome the Democratic nominees." They were treated to "a bountiful supply of everything in the market in the way of beef, pork, mutton and sugar cured hams and vegetables." The desserts included "a splendid variety of the very best cake, mountains of custards and no end to delicacies." The wives of the black Democrats had helped in the preparation. "One hundred and eighty-two men and thirty women" were present. The participation of these women was significant, since most black women in Abbeville County were stalwart Republicans.[111]

At the end of September Henderson led his men in the Lowndesville rally of "1,000 mounted men." This "grand demonstration" represented the culminating success of Democrats in recruiting and organizing black voters in Abbeville County. A large number of blacks came to see the procession which included the Abbeville Democratic "colored" band and three mounted "colored" companies captained by Henderson, Thomas Young, and G. F. Burdett, of Lowndesville, who had effectively used his group to recruit blacks. Lowndesville, described by the conservative press as a "Democratic township," drew "a more numerous colored audience than any other place." Not surprisingly, it was around then that Tom Lomax, a Republican, decided to become a Democrat.[112] By the time of the November election, Ed Henderson's club had 180 men.[113]

The Numbers Game

As students of antebellum politics have long realized, American political parties often exaggerated the number of partisans attending their rallies while they vehemently denied a large turnout for their opponents.[114] The election of 1876 was no exception. Exactly how many Red Shirts, black or white, participated in the Democratic rallies is a matter of dispute. Democrats and Republicans both played the numbers game. Democratic accounts recorded hundreds of blacks, often mounted, sometimes in red shirts, participating in Hampton rallies:

GREENVILLE (September 7)

A number of colored cavalrymen are in the procession.[115]

LAURENS (September 13)

The Colored Democratic Mounted Club 100 strong.[116]

ABBEVILLE (September 16)

Five hundred colored men were in the procession, most of whom were mounted.[117]

KINGSTREE (October 4)

Eight hundred horsemen, two hundred were "colored."[118]

SUMTER (October 7)

Over 2,000 mounted men riding in the procession, most of them wearing the red shirt, including a contingent of 300 to 400 colored men.[119]

The proportion of colored men in nearly all of the mounted clubs was about one-half.[120]

ROCK HILL (October 12)

Two hundred negroes (mounted).[121]

DUE WEST, Abbeville County (October 14)

500 black Red Shirts paraded.[122]

UNION (October 19)

The Red Shirts, with a fairly good number of colored recruits, met at the courthouse.[123]

EARLY BRANCH (October 25)

A strong club of colored Red Shirts was given a place of honor and followed directly after the campaign party as the ranks wheeled in to form the procession.[124]

WALTERBORO (October 27)

The showing of colored Democrats was one of the best, if not the best, yet seen, more than 500 of them in red shirts, riding in the parade, which included over 2,000 men, the majority on mules.[125]

CHARLESTON (c. October 31)

The Cooper River Brigade arrived in the city. They consisted of about one hundred colored Democrats and sixty white Democrats under the command of the Rev. W. H. Harleston. All were mounted [on horses and mules, mostly mules]. They hailed from the rice fields of the Cooper River, and all wore bloody shirts. They . . . disbanded and repaired to the hall of the Workingmen's

Democratic Association in Queen Street, where they organized a protracted Hampton meeting.[126]

St. George (November 2)

There were hundreds of colored men on horses, and walking about every third man was colored.[127]

For the most part, Republicans argued that the conservative press had inflated the number of persons, black and white, who attended Democratic rallies. "Half a score of hired negroes," the *Columbia Daily Union-Herald* complained, "are multiplied into a hundred enthusiastic 'respectable colored democrats.'" On September 13, the Republican newspaper contested the numbers, white and black, claimed by the conservative press for Democratic rallies at Spartanburg, Greenville, Union, and Aiken. At Spartanburg the Democrats counted 1,800 horsemen; the Republicans counted 680. The Democrats claimed "100 negroes marched in the procession" at Greenville; however, the Republicans counted 7 to 9, with 5 ending up "in the guard house for drunkenness."[128]

The Republicans scoffed at the idea that many blacks outside the Lowcountry might join the Democrats. Republican newspapers, such as the *Daily Union-Herald,* were hardly neutral observers. The *Daily,* for example, was owned by Governor Chamberlain and other important Republicans.[129] When forced to concede that as many as six hundred blacks in Charleston County might vote Democratic, the newspaper described them as "lackeys." Similarly, Richland blacks who supported the Democratic ticket were labeled "jail birds, whom the democracy have liberated, several dram drinkers, whom the democracy ply with bad whiskey, and a few fawning lackeys, barbers, and porters, to whom an occasional dime is thrown." In mid-October, the *Daily Union-Herald* claimed that conservative press accounts of "the marvelous conversions of hundreds of colored men to the democratic faith . . . in nine cases out of ten, are manufactured out of cloth." It cited as evidence an Edgefield rally attended by "1600 mounted and armed democratic horseman." There were "only nine colored men among them." Actually, the rally was a Republican meeting. Relying on such Republican sources, revisionists tend to discount the voluntary participation of blacks in Democratic processions.[130]

Privately, Republicans confirmed the growing participation of mounted blacks in Democratic parades in the Upcountry. Ralph Evans, of Chesterfield County, informed Chamberlain that fifteen black Democrats, "mounted on flashy draped horses," escorted Hampton to Cheraw. By the time they reached Cheraw, their numbers had doubled.[131] Republican newspapers grudgingly acknowledged this phenomenon. Reporting on the Democratic and Republican rallies held separately on the same day, October 18, in Abbeville, the *Daily Union-Herald* admitted that the Democratic procession had three black clubs, attired in yellow and blue shirts, "numbering about two hundred." However, it claimed: "Some of the colored men who had been inveigled into the democratic cavalry pulled off their shirts and rode over to the republican meeting. Hampton will not get two hundred colored votes in the county."[132] In early November, Republicans counted 163 blacks, mounted and on foot, at the Hampton procession in Columbia, while the Democrats claimed 208.[133] For the Charleston demonstration, the *Daily Union-Herald* reported 786 mounted men, of whom 155 were black.[134] Republicans took some consolation in the fact that not many Lowcountry blacks decided to "'jine the [Democratic] cavalry' by battalions, as was expected."[135]

Three days before the November 7 election, Republicans began to fear the worst. The *Daily Union-Herald* cited a report from H. V. Redfield. After observing the situation in Aiken, the Cincinnati journalist predicted, "If the whites can hold all these black men whom they have enrolled in democratic clubs, they will certainly carry the state." According to Redfield, "every 'colored democrat' who has joined the club and received his new hat and red shirt, and other little matters [whiskey, barbecues, pair of shoes, tobacco, etc.]" was to "be kept from backsliding." By listing a saddled horse "to ride on parade days" as "little," Redfield underestimated the Democratic strategy, perhaps even belittled it, because he did not fully appreciate the importance of parades to South Carolina communities.[136] To march, uniformed and mounted, in a procession with the community watching appealed to many South Carolinians, including ex-slaves. Perhaps the best indication that the Democrats were successfully enlisting blacks, uniformed and mounted, to march in their processions is that the Republicans adopted the tactic. A Republican rally at Darlington featured the "'Pee Dee Cooters,' a cavalry unit exceeding a hundred in number, uniformed with Hayes and Wheeler capes and caps."[137]

Profile of the Black Red Shirts

The profile of the twenty blacks identified as Red Shirts (see chart and table 1) shows how remotely they resembled the Charleston "Colored Aristocracy." They were too poor and too black. Many of them were ex-slaves who had close ties with farming and the land. Owning few possessions and illiterate, they were vulnerable to coercion and bribes. It is easy to dismiss their participation in the 1876 campaign along these lines. However, the testimonies of Asbury Green, Aaron Mitchell, and other black Red Shirt leaders reveal the paternalistic appeal Hampton had on them. Confronted with economic hard times, increasing turbulence, and Republican corruption, they sought a way out. "I will have to try another party," Green explained, "and see if they will make it no better, and if they don't don't know what in the world to do."[138]

Perhaps a closer study of the profile of these 20 blacks will give a keener insight not only into their motivations and mind-set but also into their neighborhood communities. Most were former slaves born in South Carolina. Five lived in the Midlands; the other 15 came from the Lower Piedmont counties of the Upcountry: Abbeville (4), Fairfield (7), Laurens (1), Newberry (1), and Union (2).[139] The cotton economy had made deep inroads into the region, bringing huge increases in the black population. As early as 1850, only 41.3 percent of the population in the Lower Piedmont was white. In Abbeville and Fairfield Counties, the white population was 39.3 and 33.1 percent of the total population respectively.[140] Some of these black Red Shirts from the Lower Piedmont had been the slaves of prosperous planters and lawyers. According to George Fleming of Laurens County, his master, Sam Fleming, owned a large plantation and "kept more dan 200 head of slaves." He described the plantation as a self-contained community that even manufactured its own cloth and shoes.[141] Madison Griffin remembered that his master, Billy Scott, owned seven or eight hundred acres of land, and four dozen slaves.[142] According to Frank Adamson of Fairfield County, his owner, Nicholas Peay, had bragged that "his land was ten miles square and he had a thousand slaves."[143] Thomas Campbell's master, James B. McCants, was "one of Winnsboro's first Lawyers" and a commissioner in equity for Fairfield County in the 1850s. McCants gave Campbell a red shirt to wear.[144]

Table 1
Profile of Black Red Shirts

	Yes	*No*	*No Information*	*Total*
Born in South Carolina	15	1	4	20
Born, 1850–1860	11	7	2	20
Residence, 1865–1880				
Upcountry[a]	15	5	0	20
Midlands[b]	5	15	0	20
Lowcountry	0	20	0	20
Slave before 1865	14	0	6	20
Literate	3	9	8	20
Illiterate	9	3	8	20
Black	12	3	5	20
Mulatto	3	12	6	20
Married by 1876	11	3	6	20
Married with Children by 1876	10	4[c]	6	20
Occupation, 1865–1880[d]	14	—	6	20
Artisans	2[e]	12	6	20
Domestic Workers	1[f]	13	6	20
Farming	10	4	6	20
Railroad Workers	2	12	6	20

Source: Chart.

Notes: [a]Upcountry, Lower Piedmont: Abbeville (4), Fairfield (7), Laurens (1), Newberry (1), Union (2).

[b]Midlands: Barnwell (1), Orangeburg (1), Richland (3).

[c]Married (1), Single (3).

[d]Andy Brice was counted twice as a farm and railroad laborer. Aaron Mitchell's brief tenure as town marshal was not included.

[e]Carpenter, Blacksmith-mechanic.

[f]Carriage Driver.

The hold paternalism had on some of the ex-slaves is captured in the narrative of Louisa Davis, whose husband, Sam, had been a black Red Shirt from Fairfield County. The widow was proud of her Indian heritage, "ginger cake" complexion, and "straight" hair. When she met Sam, a field hand, she was a house servant for a prominent family. "De white folks allowed us to be married on de back piazza," she recalled proudly, "and Reverend [Chalmers] Boggs performed de ceremony." Although she condemned the "white folks" for failing to give her husband a pension for serving in the

Civil War as a "bodyguard" to his master, she remained wedded to a paternalistic mind-set that embraced Franklin D. Roosevelt in the late 1930s. She attributed her house to the Democratic President. Her grandson Pinckney had managed to save the money to buy it after he had joined the Civilian Conservation Corps. She saw him as "a young warrior" working for "his chief, Mr. Roosevelt."[145]

The religious underpinnings of the paternalistic mind-set shared by conservative black South Carolinians is best expressed by Martha Lowery, the Charleston-born wife of a black Methodist Episcopal elder. She believed that Hampton had delivered her state from the turmoil of Reconstruction. "God has the right Moses at hand when the emergency comes, be it what it may," she explained. "He raised up Abraham Lincoln for that awful emergency," and "he raised up Woodrow Wilson for that world disaster in 1917." She then concluded, "He raised up Franklin D. Roosevelt for the [recent] economic disaster." The perception of Wade Hampton as a "Redeemer" was reinforced by pride in being a South Carolinian. Both husband and wife "were proud of our fine old, historic state." Martha Lowery acknowledged that "South Carolina had sometimes made mistakes, but . . . where was the state or the individual that hadn't." Sixty years after Reconstruction had ended, this black South Carolinian still asserted that Hampton had been "their friend."[146]

Planter paternalism also appealed to ex-slaves in the Midlands, which included the adjoining Orangeburg and Barnwell Counties, where Richard Mack and Joseph O'Bannon lived respectively. Richland County, where the state capitol was located, accounted for the other three black Red Shirts from the Midlands.[147] Columbia Democrats made special efforts to recruit blacks and to protect their black allies. They supported a black Democrat when he got a warrant for the arrest of a black Republican who had threatened to kill him for "desertion." At the same time, they invited independent black Republicans, like James Davis, to address their club. "If this government is to continue the same as it has been in the past," Davis announced, "I feel it that we will suffer." He exclaimed, "Colored men that are South Carolinians love South Carolina as well as you do." Davis pledged that blacks would help "drive out the carpetbagger" if the Democratic party would guarantee Wade Hampton's promises to protect their rights and to reform the government.[148]

Davis saw himself as uniquely South Carolinian, sharing with white conservatives a perception of the Yankees as outsiders. He was not atypical. On the eve of Congressional Reconstruction, a black Republican politician, Beverly Nash, noted that black South Carolinians "had grown suspicious of strangers" from the North, "adventurers with both hands open, like birds of prey." In wooing such blacks, the Democrats appealed to a common love of land and place. South Carolinians still see themselves as a unique people. Therefore, it is not surprising that the black Red Shirts would view such paternalists as Wade Hampton and Samuel McGowan as having a deeper concern and appreciation for South Carolina than New Englanders like Governor Chamberlain.[149]

Richland County was the home base of Hampton, where the general had earned his reputation as a paternalist slaveholder. His former slave, the Rev. Francis Davie, provided him with a letter of support, which the general read at various campaign stops.[150] Some Richland County black Red Shirts had been Hampton slaves. Jonas Weeks had been "raised in Mississippi" by Wade Hampton's father, who had taken him there as an infant. Weeks returned to the Columbia area in 1861. Asked by a Congressional committee member if his former master, Wade Hampton, was "a good man," he replied, "Yes." Merriman Washington, who had been "raised" by the general and knew the man not to be a "coward," named his infant son Hampton. Having been swindled by Republican trial justices, the black Red Shirt "was going to try to make it better by voting Hampton for governor." Washington led sixteen other black Red Shirts, including Jonas Weeks and Preston Taylor, to the voting polls in 1876. All three lived in the same neighborhood community, Colonel Childs's plantation. Washington, twenty-seven years old in 1876, had "never been off the place more than seven years."[151]

If James G. Thompson, editor of the *Columbia Daily Union-Herald,* were to study the profile of these twenty black Red Shirts, he might conclude that they came from "humbler" circumstances. By most traditional indices, such as literacy, occupation, property holding, and color, they were neither prosperous nor educated. Of the twelve whose literacy status is known, only three could read and write. Aaron Mitchell could read but not write. He needed "some gentleman" to renew his account books when they became too worn with wear. Pen Eubanks explained, "I ain't got no larning," while Madison Griffin stated, "We didn't learn to read and write, not allowed." Jonas Weeks was one of the few black Red Shirts who might have become literate by 1880.[152] Not well educated, their economic viability was limited. None of the four found in the 1870 Federal census reported any real or personal property. By 1876 many of the black Red Shirts were married with children to support on a modest income usually earned through agricultural work. At least ten headed families with children during Reconstruction. Of the fourteen whose postwar occupations could be determined, nine remained engaged in agriculture: five were "farm laborers," two were "farmers," and two involved in "farming." Asbury Green was a sharecropper in 1876, but the 1880 census listed him as a farm laborer. Of the remaining five, one was a carriage driver; two others were railroad hands. Andy Brice, who was one of the railroad workers, picked cotton and drove a wagon right after the war. Only two were skilled artisans after the war—blacksmith Aaron Mitchell and carpenter Edward Henderson; both had accrued unpaid bills that black clients were too poor to pay. When Mitchell became a Democrat, he noted, "Them that could pay me something won't do it." Jonas Weeks found himself in a similar dilemma. He recalled working for "a colored man" and getting nothing for his labor. If these men did not receive compensation for their work, they suffered.[153]

Of the fifteen black Red Shirts whose color could be determined, twelve were black. The other three were mulattoes.[154] The impact of color and illegitimate birth in these three men's lives illustrated how slavery, engendering divisions among South Carolina blacks, predisposed some to side with the Redeemers. Ed Barber boasted that he was "better than the full-blooded Negro." Considering himself half white and half black, he joined the whites because he knew "which side de butter was on de bread." On a trip to Charleston, Barber was rudely awakened about his feelings of superiority. When he attended St. Mark's Episcopal Church there, he felt "uncomfortable" because the generally light-skinned black congregation "was too 'hifalootin' in de ways." They were more affluent and better educated, many of them free persons of color. Ironically, he jeered at how they "bow and scrape and ape de white folks."[155]

John C. Brown, who described himself as "yallow," had been told that his mother "was a white lady dat visited my old marster and mistress." Tom Dawkins, a Fairfield County planter, found him "dressed in nice baby clothes" and abandoned in a basket near a railroad in Dawkins, South Carolina. After the war the carriage driver on the Dawkins place informed Brown that he was his father. The black stepmother, who was apparently abusive to the youth, caused the fourteen-year-old to run away to Robert Clowney's place, where he met his future wife. He "followed Marse Robert Clowney in politics, wore a red shirt, and voted for him to go to de Legislature."[156] Abbeville Red Shirt Edward Henderson was so light-skinned that a member of the Congressional committee asked: "You are not a colored man, are you?" Henderson's white grandmother was of the South Carolina Laurens family. His white father, Francis Henderson Jr., had been born in Great Britain. A bachelor, his father had boarded with the McClaren family of Abbeville. Ed Henderson's mother, Hattie McClaren, was a slave of John McClaren, who "raised" him. His father died unmarried. Had Ed Henderson been white and considered legitimate, he would have inherited a sizable estate.[157]

Born in the 1850s, many of the twenty black Red Shirts were children of the war. At least eleven had been born during the decade before the Civil War. "I 'members very little 'bout de war," Andy Brice declared, "tho' I was a good size boy when de Yankees come." Thus, few of the twenty related in any detail their occupations as slaves. Of the seven who did, four worked in the fields before the war ended, and one was a house servant. The remaining two, Richard Mack and Joe O'Bannon, were body servants during the war, as was the field hand Sam Davis. Thomas Campbell of Fairfield County was only six years old when the war began. The house servant never knew who his father was. "My white folks was all de parents I had," he declared, "and me wid a skin as black as ink. My belly was always full of what they had and I never suffer from clothes on my back or shoes on my feets." Perhaps lacking a vivid memory of the harshness of antebellum slavery, this younger generation may have been more susceptible to the postwar paternalism of Hampton.[158] Of the seven black Red Shirts who testified before the Congressional committee in Columbia, four (Asbury Green, Tom Lomax, Aaron Mitchell, and Merriman Washington) had been Republicans who became Democrats. Preston Taylor, as well as Lomax, Mitchell, and Washington, became a Democrat in 1876. Disillusioned by the economic hard times and corruption under Republican rule, these black Red Shirts found Hampton's paternalism appealing. "I would be willing to die with Hampton any day," Washington exclaimed.[159]

The war had bred anti-Yankee bitterness among some of the ex-slaves, particularly one whose father had fought for the Confederacy. Charlie Jeff Harvey's father had joined the Holcombe Legion of Union County. He was wounded at the Second Battle of Manassas and again, this time almost mortally, at Kingston, North Carolina. Unable to function, he was dismissed from the army. Charlie Harvey was left to care for both his mother and wounded father. Times were very hard. He remembered, "For about four o[r] five years after the Confederate War, we had very little to eat. We had given everything we could to the soldiers." The suffering so embittered him that he subsequently joined the Ku Klux Klan in Union County. He described how the Klan drowned blacks in the Broad River because they had been issued bullets "under carpetbag rule" from Gov. Robert K. Scott during Reconstruction.[160] Some black Red Shirts, such as Madison Griffin, never forgot the destruction Lincoln and the Yankees had wrought. "I think Abe Lincoln might ter done good," the ex-slave conceded, "but he had us all scared to death, took our mules and burned our places." Griffin was about twelve years old when the war had ended.[161]

Raised in a hierarchical society, some of the black Red shirts shared the class and anti-Yankee bias of their former owners. "Every Yankee I see had de stamp of poor white trash on them," Andy Brice asserted. He resented the way some of the Union soldiers treated the women of both races. "They strutted 'round, big lke fashion, a bustin' in rooms widout knockin', talkin' free to de white ladies, and familiar to de slave gals, ransakin' drawers, and runnin' deir bayonets into feather beds, and into de flower beds in de yards."[162] Similarly, George Fleming of Laurens County had nothing but disgust for white Republican Joe Crews, a former slave trader, "and other scalawags like him." Crews, who headed Republican Party efforts in the county, served in the legislature. For this young Democrat, such men "had done made all de money dey could off selling niggers, so dey thought dey could make some more by making 'greements wid de Republicans."[163]

George Fleming blamed these Republican "scalawags," especially Crews, for the killing of his father, William Fleming. Before the October election of 1870, the parties in Laurens County were already polarized along race lines. As chairman of the county board of election managers, Crews began organizing companies of black militia. Some of their weapons, provided by the state government, were stored in the town of Laurens at Crews's place, known as Tin Pot Alley. In response, whites purchased Winchester rifles, as many as eighty to one hundred. Tensions resulting from an incident in nearby Newberry County spread to Laurens County. Despite a near confrontation between the races, the election, however, took place peacefully enough. Trouble occurred the day after the election, when throngs of people came to town for Court Day. A constable and a white man got into a "row," and a pistol went off, some fifty yards from Tin Pot Alley. An irate white mob stormed the building, killing at least two blacks; one of them was George Fleming's father.[164]

Anger and bitterness, perhaps even feelings of guilt and self-hate, may have blurred George Fleming's memory when he related his father's death sixty-seven years later. Fleming, sixteen at the time, recalled participating in the Tin Pot Alley riot as a Red Shirt: "Us Democrats broke in de storehouse in Tin Pot Alley and got every one of dem guns. De niggers names was on de stock of de guns. We sho had a hot time when dem niggers come up dar trying to vote. Dat's when my daddy got kil't." However, the riot occurred in 1870, before the appearance of the Red Shirts.[165] By 1876, when Fleming joined the Red Shirts, Crews was dead; he had been assassinated in 1875.[166] Blaming the Republican "scalawag" for recruiting his father, George Fleming rationalized: "My daddy, Bill, was bullheaded. He done got dem ideas in his head and he said he gwine to vote fer de Republicans in spite of hell."[167]

An increasing number of ex-slaves hoped Hampton's election would bring an end to terrorism against themselves and their families. Violence against blacks mounted almost from the very beginning of Radical Reconstruction. Klan activity reached epidemic proportions after the 1870 election. Women and children found themselves helpless victims as white terrorists broke into their homes to seize the guns of black militia members and to keep black males from voting Republican. One black Red Shirt, Madison Griffin of Newberry County, vividly recalled how the Klan summarily dealt with "bad niggers."[168] Lacking Federal protection in particularly violent counties, like Laurens and Barnwell, some black Republicans informed Governor Chamberlain that if he did not send in troops, they would be "obliged to join the Democratic clubs for protection."[169] Families split over the election of 1876. William Pratt of Chester County recalled that his brother turned down requests to join the Red Shirts, but his brother-in-law "joined and wore one of the shirts with them. He wanted Wade Hampton elected as he believed it was best for us. He was a Democrat and said they all ought to wear them." Voting for Hampton seemed the safest way to restore peace.[170]

Red Shirt Terrorism and Federal Intervention

The inability of the Federal government to protect South Carolina Republicans took its toll, as Upcountry blacks were whipped and terrorized. Bouregard Corry, of Union County, related how the Red Shirts took his father out of his house and whipped him. Likewise, Silas Glenn, of Newberry County, remembered: "The Ku Klux and Red Shirts didn't like negroes. They would catch them and whip them." Even Democratic supporters conceded that some white Red Shirts were "reckless and dangerous men whose instinct was violence."[171] Not surprisingly, an elderly black woman, mesmerized by a long procession of Red Shirts marching in Anderson, fled in fear. "I never will forget the look of wild, awful terror on her face," a white Red Shirt boasted with glee, "as she dashed almost under our horses' feet, into the woods, followed by the shouts of the company."[172]

Presented with evidence of increased violence against black voters, Governor Chamberlain ordered the rifle clubs disbanded on October 7. Some of the clubs, like the Richland Rifle Club, eventually heeded his command.[173] Others disingenuously reorganized as social groups, calling themselves brass bands and baseball clubs or, more outrageously, church sewing circles and "Mother's Little Helpers."[174] These clubs were becoming a serious political liability to Hampton, as the Republicans highlighted every example of intimidation to advocate greater Federal intervention. In mid-October, a *New York Times* correspondent alerted Northern readers to a "Reign of Terror" on black Republicans in Barnwell and Aiken Counties.[175] On October 17, President Ulysses S. Grant, declaring a "state of insurrection" in South Carolina, issued a Proclamation charging "all persons engaged in said unlawful and insurrectionary proceedings to disperse." More significantly, he ordered additional Federal troops be sent to South Carolina.[176]

Federal troops were eventually stationed in Abbeville County at

Greenwood and Ninety-Six. Their presence stabilized the situation somewhat. According to one Republican planter, Red Shirts who had intimidated blacks in his neighborhood were subsequently caught and indicted for their activities.[177] But the presence of the men in blue fed the fears of white conservatives. Wildly false rumors spread quickly, suggesting how potentially explosive the imminent election was becoming. The *Abbeville Medium,* encouraging its readers to keep calm, reported as untrue stories that "United States soldiers compelled a colored democrat to pull off his red shirt." Saturday night and Sunday before the election, the silence in the town of Abbeville "was nearly oppressive." On Monday "'Honest Joe' beat the long roll for the Democrats at the Court House." Election day in the town passed by peacefully enough. However, even after the election, the fears and anxieties did not subside. On the Saturday afterwards, the townspeople were agitated by rumors that Union troops and disgruntled Republicans were preparing "for a general slaughter of the white people with their colored allies for out-voting them." It was just the Federal troops departing for Florida.[178]

On November 8, the *Abbeville Medium* reported that "Honest Joe," who had "been working for Hampton ever since the campaign opened," had been driven out of his home by his mother "because he saw fit to be honest and respectable. The white people are determined to take care of all such allies."[179]

Black Red Shirts and the Response of Black Republicans

Facing greater Federal intervention and the possibility that a Hampton victory might be overturned because of violence against blacks, the Democrats took special efforts to feature black cavalrymen riding alongside their white counterparts. Their presence blunted charges that white conservatives were totally anti-black. The conservative press highlighted blacks' participation. Reporting a Sumter rally, the *Charleston News and Courier* claimed: "There was no distinction of color in any part of the programme or proceedings. The whole number of whites and blacks seemingly was about equal. The proportion of colored men in nearly all of the mounted clubs was about one-half. . . . They rode side by side with their white friends and drowned their less practiced voices in every 'Hurrah for Hampton' that was given."[180] The same newspaper counted hundreds of mounted men, blacks and whites, at a Kingstree rally; it found "no distinction on account of race or color or previous condition. White cavalrymen and colored cavalrymen rode side by side." Furthermore, "a sturdy American Democrat of African descent headed one of the cavalry companies with a banner which represented a colored man in the act of kicking a white brother, who bore on his shoulders a carpet-bag." The inscription on the banner read: "Things are too hot for carpetbaggers. Let us go, boys!"[181] The black Red Shirt Aaron Mitchell played a similar role as the "Vulcan of the colored Democracy" at a Hampton rally in Abbeville. He carried a transparency depicting "a carpet-bagger leaving in haste with bag and umbrella in hand, with the inscription 'Home Again'; 2nd side 'Down with carpetbaggers'; Down with scalawags.'"[182] Republicans attributed such black support to intimidation. In Greenville County a black Republican official claimed that many blacks were being "compelled to buy red shirts, declare themselves as democrats to save their lives."[183]

However, as Hampton built up black support, some of it obviously voluntary, black Democrats became the target of black Republicans. As early as September 6, the *Abbeville Medium* reported that "radical negroes" were continually harassing Ed Henderson and other black Democratic organizers. Although Henderson was asked to leave town, much of the harassment consisted of social ostracism, such as threatening to expel black Democrats from the churches.[184] But sometimes the threats were more physical. S. L. Hutchens, a black lawyer originally from Georgia, stumped the state for the Democrats. Hutchens reported that on a visit to Camden, he was threatened with a knife by a black man named Frederic McCoy. "Every democratic nigger ought to have his throat cut," McCoy declared.[185] Another black Democratic stump speaker, John Lee of Richland County, also recalled being threatened by McCoy at Camden.[186] Fellow Richland County black Democrat Philip Grandison was knocked unconscious by a brick.[187] One night the home of Aaron Mitchell in Abbeville County was approached by more than fifty Republicans, one screaming, "Here's the damn democrat's house." Cursing him and hollering, they fired two pistol shots at the house during the night. Mitchell's wife, Frances, was terrified. "I can't help it," he told her. "I can't go out."[188] The conservative press claimed that many blacks would join the movement "but are deterred from it from fear of personal violence." The black women were particularly "bitter in their opposition."[189]

Black Women as Political Participants

The Republicans could count on black women to participate in their campaigns. The women attended mass rallies, prepared meals for the participants, danced, sang "spirituals," arranged the stands, and rode in processions. Some of them were from an emerging black middle class. At a Winnsboro rally, young black women cooked the dinner and decorated the stand. "Dressed in white, with pink sashes across the breast, bearing the name of Chamberlain in large letters," they sang campaign songs, including the well-known "Hold the Fort." Ladies who belonged to "the elite of colored society in Columbia" rode in carriages during a torchlight procession for Chamberlain.[190]

As much as the conservative press lauded white women for their involvement in the Hampton cause, it criticized black women who engaged in Republican politics, sometimes labeling them "negro wenches." Some black women protested to Wade Hampton that the Democrats would not allow them to wear "hoop skirts." While white women were able to confirm their true womanhood by participating in the political process, black women were not allowed the same consideration, especially the poorer ones, who did all in their power to keep black men from voting Democratic.[191] Lacking suffrage, facing economic hard times, and told by Republicans that a Democratic victory could mean the re-enslavement of themselves and their children, these "humbler" women felt compelled to take direct action against black men they considered traitors to the race. They stigmatized such men as unmanly and took the war into the home. Richard Roman found the women a "heap worse" than the men.[192] Black Red Shirt Asbury Green of Abbeville County agreed that the black women were "just like a rattlesnake." They tried to persuade his wife, Mary, to take the couple's five children and to leave him.[193] John Lee reported that in Columbia three black women from the country actually tore the red shirt off a black man marching in a Democratic procession. Others informed

Lee's wife that he "was voting to put her and her children back into slavery." They told him, "Your wife ought to be burned out for living with you." Shouting "damned old Lee" ought to be killed, they threw "their clothes clean up to their heads and made such a noise."[194] Tom Lomax and fellow black Democrats of Lowndesville, Abbeville County, were also confronted by black women, who pulled up their coats and told them "to kiss their arse."[195] In defending their breadbaskets, these women employed tactics that black rice laborers used in the much publicized riot or strike along the Combahee River in the summer of 1876. The workers succeeded in part because they boldly and violently intimidated black strikebreakers. Ironically, the women, at times, resorted to abuse that white men had inflicted on them.[196]

Like the *sans-coulottes* in the French Revolution, many of these black women were set apart by the "pantelets" and "breeches" they wore in the fields, doing the same work as the men. "Couldn't tell 'em apart in de field," recalled one ex-slave.[197] During Reconstruction these were the women black and white Democrats alike labeled as not "ladylike." When so accused, one of them shouted: "I am down on these damned democratic niggers."[198] In encouraging the *pantelets,* Republican leaders furthered the rift. According to Democratic lawyer William D. Simpson, Republican Joe Crews urged the black women in 1870 to "dress as a man and vote."[199] Black Red Shirt Andy Brice claimed, "Colored preachers so 'furiate de women, dat they would put on breeches and vote de 'Publican radical ticket" in 1878.[200] Not surprisingly, these women labeled the loyal wives of black Democrats "dirty bitches."[201]

Not all the wives of black Democrats stood by their husbands. Jonas Weeks recalled how Richland County black women abused him for being a Democrat: "They would pull off my breeches and call me a devil." His wife, Winnie, cursed him and refused to give him clean shirts.[202] According to a Republican newspaper, a Richland County woman demanded that her husband publicly recant his support for Hampton. He did so in front of four hundred people because "his wife had refused to sleep with him," and he desired to "enjoy the society of his family and be reconciled on the coming Sabbath."[203] The militancy of these black women was having such an impact on the upcoming election that in late September, the *Abbeville Medium* complained: "The negro women at Due West are terribly bitter in their hostility to the white people and refuse to have anything to do with their husbands if they join the Democratic clubs." The paper recommended that "the best and surest cure for all this is to cut off their supplies and refuse to give them any employment."[204]

On election day the women continued their efforts with a vengeance. In Richland County, when black Democrat Merriman Washington led his sixteen black Red Shirts to the polls, black women "stripped some of [his] boys of their red shirts at the polls." Only eight voted.[205] When Preston Taylor, one of these eight, left the polls, shouting "Hurrah for Hampton," these women "jumped on [him] and tore off [his] clothes. . . . Right at the box where the voting was." They left him naked.[206] In Abbeville County, where the Democrats organized at least three active black clubs, the women were especially abusive. At the courthouse, they were "abusing and going on terrible." Aaron Mitchell asked that the town marshal keep them from the polls. He reported that some black Democrats somehow managed to slip away from their wives and the other black women to vote.[207] Declaiming the women's behavior on election day as "unseemly" and "SCANDALOUS," the *Abbeville Medium* pronounced: "Such filth and immodest conduct it has never been our bad luck to see before."[208]

Edward Henderson agreed: "The colored women was the worst of all. I have been rebuked a good deal by them through the county." Women tried to keep men from joining his club by saying "they would starve them; and that they wouldn't sleep in the same bed with them." One wife threw her husband's clothes out of the house and locked the door. One light-skinned black, who lived with General McGowan and wanted to vote for him, was whipped in the street by his wife. Henderson's wife, Harriett, was threatened with a whipping at church; his ten-year-old daughter, Mahala, was whipped at school. The guilty parties were eventually arrested.[209]

The Republican press put a different spin on such activities: "Edward Henderson, of Abbeville, notifies the colored women that he will be down upon them with the full penalties of the law if they try to abuse or intimidate the members of his democratic club. Poor fellows, the girls must not frighten them."[210] In defending Henderson, the conservative press claimed, "The negro wenches, who make their living by prostituting their persons, are especially active against him."[211] The Republican press, in turn, acclaimed the steadfastness of black women. While "the white ladies urged the democrats to vote for the conquering hero, with the usual smiles and blandishments; the humbler colored women threatened their lords divorce from bed and board if they did." The day after the election, the *Columbia Daily Union-Herald* proclaimed: "The colored women fought nobly."[212]

Impact of the Black Conservative Vote: Abbeville County

It is nearly impossible to measure with any precision the impact that black conservatives, particularly the black Red Shirts, had on the outcome of the 1876 election. Fraud and intimidation were so widespread that any voter analysis is fraught with difficulties. Republicans claimed Chamberlain beat Hampton by 3,145 votes; Democrats asserted Chamberlain lost by 1,134 votes. A conservative black lawyer estimated that 10,000 blacks voted Democratic. Chamberlain thought only 3,000 had; Hampton suggested 17,000. Probably the total was around 5,000, about the same as the number of whites who had voted Republican at the peak of Reconstruction.[213] It is even more difficult to determine how many of these blacks voted for the Democratic ticket voluntarily. Some white conservatives felt that the effort spent on courting the black vote, while earnest and persevering, did not really influence the results. They believed intimidation carried the day.[214] Revisionists, like Joel Williamson, argued that much of the conservative effort was focused not on wooing the black voters but on keeping them "away from the polls."[215] However, if Hampton did beat Chamberlain 92,261 to 91,127, with a margin of 1,134 as claimed by the Democrats, his campaign to persuade black voters might have made a difference.

Martha Lowery, a free person of color from Charleston who taught in South Carolina during Reconstruction, believed that Hampton's election "was brought about mostly by ex-slaves." They deserved the credit for ending a "carpetbag regime" full of "graft" and "confusion." She recalled, "At that time there was plenty signs that the leadership of the South intended to make full citizens of the Negroes and live in accord with them."[216]

Perhaps it is best to examine the election results of an Upcountry county such as Abbeville, where the Democrats simultaneously terrorized and wooed black voters. Although the Democrats were more successful in recruiting blacks in Abbeville County than elsewhere in the Upcountry, race relations were far from idyllic there. Republicans ranked Abbeville alongside Aiken, Edgefield, Barnwell, and Laurens as prime examples of Democratic fraud.[217] But the Abbeville experience, although not typical, was probably representative of the methods that the Democrats employed throughout the state.

While in Abbeville County nearly 500 blacks (478 out of 4,951) failed to vote in the election of 1876, they still outnumbered white voters, by 4,473 to 3,077. Despite this black majority, Wade Hampton carried Abbeville County over Chamberlain, 3,852 to 3,669. Of the 16 precincts with election returns, Chamberlain won 5. These 5 had large black majorities: Abbeville No. 2, Calhoun's Mills, Ninety-Six, Smithville, and White Hall. Assuming that all 3,077 whites voted for Hampton, then at least 775 blacks (about 17.3 percent of black voters) cast their ballots for Hampton.[218] Republicans conceded that about 20 percent of the black vote in Abbeville County went Democratic.[219]

Intimidation, especially in the country precincts, certainly played a significant role.[220] Republican politicians related in detail how they were unable to canvass the county safely before the election.[221] Probably the two precincts most affected by Democratic fraud and intimidation were Magnolia and Calhoun's Mills, both black strongholds. There were no returns from Magnolia, because the night before the election some twenty-five Red Shirts destroyed the ballot box there, forcing the voters to cast their ballots at Calhoun's Mills and other precincts.[222] The Democratic intimidation at Calhoun's Mills was so bad that at least 150 Republicans failed to vote. Both Lewis Clay and William H. Heard, black Republicans who were running for office, substantiated the impact of the intimidation. Since the Republican ticket was red, the community knew how individuals voted.[223] The intimidation and fraud may have kept Republicans away, but such tactics did not result in more black voters for Hampton. Most likely, only 43 out of 515 blacks in the precinct (or 8.3 percent) voted for Hampton.[224]

The Democrats were most successful in wooing black voters in precincts with active black Democratic clubs. In Lowndesville, out of 625 voters (266 white and 359 black), Hampton won 446 ballots, probably 180 of them from blacks.[225] The day after the election, the *Abbeville Medium* con-

Table 2
Returns for South Carolina Governor by Precinct, Abbeville County, November 7, 1876

	Hampton	*Chamberlain*	*White Voters*	*Black Voters*	*Black Hampton Voters*[a]	*% Black Hampton Voters*[d]
Abbeville 1	457	335	345	448	112	25.0
Abbeville 2	9	432	2	440	7	1.6
Calhoun's Mills	243	467	200	515	43	8.3
St. Charlotte	286	79	225	142	61	43.0
Cokesbury	324	290	276	339	48	14.2
Greenwood	574	361	453	483	121	25.1
Ninety-Six	8	345	6	354	2	0.6
Donaldsville	224	95	202	118	22	18.6
Due West	298	138	249	187	49	26.2
Antreville	229	178	208	199	21	10.6
Chiles'X Roads	220	53	172	101	48	47.5
Smithville	103	291	99	295	4	1.4
Lowndesville	446	173	266	359	180	50.1
Magnolia[b]						
White Hall	79	212	74	218	5	2.3
Long Cane	132	112	129	118	3	2.5
Cedar Springs	220	108	171	157	49	31.2
Total	3,852	3,669	3,077[c]	4,473	775	17.3

SOURCE: "Vote of Abbeville County at the General Election, November 7th, 1876," *Abbeville Medium,* November 15, 1876. The official returns as reported in *South Carolina in 1876,* 3: 578, were the same.

NOTES: [a]Black Hampton voters estimated by subtracting white voters from the total Hampton vote.

[b]Magnolia reported no returns.

[c]The newspaper total was mistakenly given as 3,095.

[d]Percent of total black vote.

gratulated club leader Thomas Young, who "carried more colored votes on Tuesday than any other man in the county." He claimed he recruited the votes of 161 blacks.[226] Similarly, in Abbeville No. 1, some 112 blacks voted for Hampton. Aaron Mitchell and Edward Henderson helped deliver the black vote. Mitchell told a Congressional committee that he "voted" some one to two hundred blacks at the Abbeville courthouse.[227]

Having done "their duty," the black Democrats of Due West celebrated with "a splendid dinner." At least a quarter of the blacks voting in the precinct had cast their ballot for Hampton.[228] Such support elated conservatives. The *Abbeville Medium* was especially ecstatic. Its co-editor, Robert Hemphill, led all the other candidates in the race for the state house of representatives. Colonel Cothran won his race for solicitor, eighth circuit. "We Must Keep Our Pledges with the Colored People," the *Medium* intoned. Estimating that there were six to eight hundred black conservatives in the county, the paper advised employers to hire them first and raise their wages to "show them the pledges of the campaign are binding, and that what we said in the heat of the canvass we mean to carry out."[229] The *Marion Star,* located in the Pee Dee area of the Upcountry, endorsed the *Medium* editorial.[230] The conservative press understood that some of their black supporters were willing to give the Democrats a chance but, if dissatisfied, would vote them out of office in a subsequent election. Blacks, like Ed Butler of Cokesbury, had made it clear that they planned to split their tickets because they did not want to lose their "connection with the Republican party."[231] The *Star* counseled: "Our good will to them must not be measured in days or months but must extend through years until we shall secure forever the good results of our triumph."[232]

Aftermath: Revising History

The black Red Shirts gave credibility to Wade Hampton's victory in a hotly contested election marred by fraud and intimidation. Edward Henderson and six other black Red Shirts dutifully supported him at the 1876 Congressional hearings in Columbia. As partisan Democrats, they never acknowledged any conservative violence against Republicans. In 1877, a grateful governor appointed Henderson a jury commissioner for the Abbeville area.

In 1878 Hampton's re-election was a foregone conclusion. He had virtually no Republican opposition. However, there were still Republican strongholds at the county level. Moreover, despite Hampton's protests, Gary and his associates, such as George Tillman, adopted a "white line policy." In a speech at a September rally in Barnwell County, Tillman attributed the failure of the Democrats in 1876 to carry certain counties in the east and south to the liberality of the Hampton plan. He vowed conservatives would not let this happen again.[233]

In the 1878 campaign Red Shirts were active in counties such as Fairfield and Barnwell. For example, one thousand mounted men attended a September rally in Winnsboro, Fairfield County. Most of them wore red shirts. The reporter also noted that "one-fourth of the riders were colored." In November Andy Brice, who had worn the red shirt in 1876, was present when white Democrats violently blocked Republicans from voting at Woodward, Fairfield County.[234] A month earlier a disturbing incident involving black Democrats occurred in Barnwell County. On October 11, some black Democrats armed with pistols joined white Red Shirts in disrupting a Republican meeting at Blackville in that county. The U.S. commissioner at Blackville issued scores of warrants against black Democrats, including Osceola Gantt of Barnwell County. Fred Nix Jr., chairman of the Barnwell County Republican Party, swore in an affidavit that Gantt had "intimidated him in his advocacy of [black Republican] Robert Smalls for Congress." One observer at the Blackville rally bragged that Smalls would "dream for some time of the Red-shirt colored men he saw here to-day." Gantt and sixteen other defendants appeared at the United States District Court in Charleston in October. The judge ordered the jury to acquit them because the government failed to prove that Nix was prevented from voting because of his color. Both Nix and Gantt were black. When the November elections concluded, all counties in South Carolina except Beaufort went Democratic.[235]

The legacy of the black Red Shirts barely survived Hampton's re-election. Only one year later, at an Abbeville rally, when the governor reiterated his support for the rights of blacks, the "white audience" booed and hissed. The mood of white conservative voters in South Carolina had changed. Abbeville Democrats narrowly voted not to accept Edward Henderson's company as an independent club. The blacks had to join the white club.[236] Although a handful of black Democrats, like Pen Eubanks, were allowed to vote in the Democratic primary well into the twentieth century,[237] racial demagogues such as Benjamin Tillman revised history. At a 1909 Red Shirt reunion in Anderson, Tillman not only laid claim to the Red Shirt legacy for his family, he also left the black Red Shirts entirely out. Asserting the importance of his brother George, Tillman stressed the role terror had played.[238]

In September 1911 when aging Red Shirts assembled in the state capital for their annual reunion, Gov. Cole Blease told the gathering how he had proudly worn the red shirt as a youth.[239] The legacy was being passed on; the youngest Red Shirt in the parade for this reunion was eight-year-old William M. Bostwick of Barnwell. Ironically, among the thousand paraders were four black Democrats, including "Uncle Joe" O'Bannon from Barnwell. Dressed in a red shirt, astride a mule, this ex-slave could briefly relive the glory days of 1876, when he with hundreds of other Red Shirts joined Wade Hampton in a cavalcade through Barnwell County. By printing a photograph of O'Bannon, the *Columbia State* highlighted the role he and other black Red Shirts played: "The good he helped to bring about is still bearing fruit."[240]

Twenty-seven years later, the same newspaper pictured U.S. Senator "Cotton Ed" Smith celebrating his re-nomination, surrounded by a new generation of white Red Shirts, expressing "the spirit of 1876." Smith had defeated Franklin D. Roosevelt's friend, Gov. Olin D. Johnson.[241] In contrast, black Red Shirt Frank Adamson saw no inconsistency in supporting two patrician Democrats, Wade Hampton in 1876 and Franklin D. Roosevelt in 1937: "I'll be . . . hollerin' for Mr. Roosevelt, just as loud as I holler then for Hampton."[242]

Hampton never envisioned allowing blacks to exercise any real authority in shaping the ideology of the Democratic Party. But given the trajectory of ten years of Republican rule and the political realities of 1876, Hampton seemed to offer his black supporters an alternative to a national Republican Party on the verge of ending Radical Reconstruction no matter what the outcome would be in South Carolina. His prestige in the state was probably second only to Robert E. Lee's. Highly prizing both his word and honor, Hampton promised to preserve two of Radical Reconstruction's most important gains: the suffrage and public education. Viewed from the waning years of the twentieth century, the decision of these blacks to support Hampton, particularly those who donned uniforms and marched in the processions shouting "Hurrah for Hampton," seems at best short-sighted or naive.

Perhaps it is more fruitful to view these black Red Shirts as nineteenth-century South Carolinians who saw politics as a way of bettering themselves and their families. Of course, bribery, as well as economic and physical coercion, influenced a large percentage to varying degrees. Some were opportunists who wanted to take advantage of the conservative tide in the state. Wearing a red shirt offered them status, patronage, or at least the promise of a continued paternalism. But others sincerely thought Hampton would bring peace, prosperity, and honest government. As the testimonies and narratives suggest, the black Red Shirts often had mixed motives. However, the increasing hostility of the black Republicans, especially the women, and their church congregations indicated that black Red Shirt leaders such as Edward Henderson and Aaron Mitchell were effective in winning black voters to Hampton's cause. Sixty years later Richard Mack and other black Red Shirts thought they had made a difference. They remained proud of their involvement in the campaign of 1876. In 1937, Pen Eubanks exclaimed: "Us had done 'lected Marse Hampton as de new governor of South Ca'linia."[243]

CHART:

Hampton's Black Red Shirts

Name	Place/Date Of Birth	Residence To 1865	 1865-1880
Adamson, Frank #*^	SC (1855)	Fairfield Co., SC	Township No. 5 Fairfield Co., SC
Barber, Charley #*	Near Great Falls Chester Co., SC (1856)	Probably Chester Co., SC	Winnsboro Fairfield Co., SC (1876)
Barber, Ed #*+	12 miles east of Winnsboro Fairfield Co., SC (1860)	12 miles east of Winnsboro Fairfield Co., SC	Township No. 5 Fairfield Co., SC
Brice, Andy #*	SC (1856)		Woodward Fairfield Co., SC (1878) Township No. 2 Fairfield Co., SC (1880)
Brown, John C. #*	Dawkins Fairfield Co., SC (1852)	Probably Fairfield Co., SC	Probably Fairfield Co., SC
Campbell, Thomas #*	Horeb Section Fairfield Co., SC (1855)	Fairfield Co., SC	Probably Fairfield Co., SC
Davis, Sam #*+			Probably Fairfield Co., SC
Eubanks, Pen *+	(1854)		Probably Union Union Co., SC
Fleming, George #*	Near Laurens Laurens Co., SC (1854)	Near Laurens Laurens Co., SC	Cross Hill Township Laurens Co., SC

Occupation					
To 1865	*1865-1880*	*Color*	*Literacy*	*Marital Status to 1876*	*Sources*
icked Cotton	Farmer (1880)	B	L (1880)	MC	1a, 4b, 5a, 7c
	Railroad Hand			Probably S	1b, 7f
	Farmer (1880)	MU	IL (1880)	S	1c, 5b
icked Cotton (?)	Picked Cotton Wagon Driver Railroad Laborer (1880)	B	IL (1880)	Probably S	1e, 5c
		MU		MC	1f, 3, 7d
Iouse and Office ervant	Carriage Driver	B			1g, 7c
ield Hand ody Servant uring the War				M	1h, 7b
			Probably IL		1i, 7e
ield Hand		B			1j, 4a

Name	Place/Date Of Birth	Residence: To 1865	Residence: 1865-1880
Green, Asbury #*+	SC (1849)		Hodges Depot Abbeville Co., SC (1876) Cokesbury Township Abbeville Co., SC (1880)
Griffin, Madison #*	SC (1853)		Cromers Township No.4 Newberry Co., SC
Henderson, Edward #***+	SC (1828)	Abbeville Abbeville Co., SC	Abbeville Abbeville Co., SC
Jones, Jack *+			Probably Union Co., SC
Lomax, Tom **+	SC (1851)		Lowndesville Abbeville Co., SC (1876) Long Cane Township Abbeville Co., SC (1880)
Mack, Richard #*+	Limestone, VA (1833)	Probably Orangeburg Co., SC	Probably Orangeburg Co., SC
Mitchell, Aaron ***+	SC (1816)		Abbeville Abbeville Co., SC
O'Bannon, Joe *+	SC (1827)	Probably Barnwell Co., SC	Barnwell Barnwell Co., SC
Taylor, Preston *	(1853)		Near Columbia Richland Co., SC
Washington, Merriman #*	SC (1849)	Probably Richland Co., SC	Near Columbia Richland Co., SC
Weeks, Jonas #*	SC (1846)	Mississippi/SC	Near Columbia Richland Co., SC

Symbols: #Slave !Free Person of Color +Mounted ^On Foot

Date of Birth: Determined first by the testimonies of the blacks themselves, then the Federal cens

Color: Black (B) or Mulatto (MU) as indicated in the Federal census or in the testimonies of the blacks and their interviewers.

Literacy: The ability to read and write. Literate ((L); Illiterate (IL). Note that this was often determined through the Federal census, which was not always accurate.

Occupation					
To 1865	*1865-1880*	*Color*	*Literacy*	*Marital Status to 1876*	*Sources*
	Farmer [Sharecropper] (1876) Farm Laborer (1880)	B	IL (1880)	MC	2b, 5i
	Farm Laborer (1880)	B	IL (1880)	MC	1k, 5f
	Carpenter (1876) (1880)	MU	IL (1880)	MC	2c, 5h, 6a1, 6a4, 6b, 7a
					1i, 7e
	Farming (1876) (1880)	B	IL (1880)	MC	2d, 5d, 6a3
ody Servant uring the War		B			1d, 7g
	Town Marshal (1870) Blacksmith/ Mechanic (1876)	B	IL (1870)	MC	2e, 4e, 6a1, 6a2, 6b, 6d, 7a
ody Servant uring thc War	Farm Laborer (1870)	B	IL (1870)	MC	4c, 6c
	Farming (1876)				2a, 2f
	Farm Laborer (1876) (1880)	B	L (1880)	MC	2a, 5e
	Farm Laborer (1870) Farmer (1876) [Farm?] Laborer (1880)	B	IL (1870) IL (1876) L (1880)	MC	2a, 2g, 4d, 5g

MARITAL STATUS: Married (M), Married with Child/Children (MC), or Single (S). It was assumed that persons (the man listed first, the woman second) in the same household in 1870 and near the same age were married. The age of the eldest child in the household was used to determine if the couple were married before 1876.

UNIFORM: *Red **Yellow ***Blue

Chart Sources

1. Ten slave narratives are in the United States Work Projects Administration (WPA) Collection, Federal Writers' Project: Slave Narrative Project, Slave Narratives, South Carolina, vol. 14, parts 1-4, in the Manuscript Division of the Library of Congress, Washington, D.C. (part and page numbers cited below); George Fleming's narrative is in the WPA Federal Writers' Project Papers, Ex-Slave Narratives, of the South Caroliniana Library, University of South Carolina, Columbia.

a. 14: pt. 1, 13-16 (Adamson).

b. 14: pt. 1, 29-33 (Barber, C.).

c. 14: pt. 1, 34-37 (Barber, E.).

d. 14: pt. 3, 151-156 (Mack).

e. 14: pt. 1, 75-79 (Brice).

f. 14: pt. 1, 127-130 (Brown).

g. 14: pt. 1, 176-179 (Campbell).

h. 14: pt. 1, 299-303 (Davis).

i. 14: pt. 2, 27-29 (Eubanks) (Jones).

j. South Caroliniana Library (Fleming).

k. 14: pt. 2, 212-214 (Griffin).

2. U.S. Congress, Senate, *South Carolina in 1876: Testimony as to the Denial of the Elective Franchise in South Carolina at the Elections of 1875 and 1876*, 44th Cong., 2d sess., S. Misc. Doc. 48 (Washington, D.C.: Government Printing Office, 1877), vols. 1 (Serial 1727), 2 (Serial 1728).

a. 1: 562-565, 591-592 (Washington). Washington, who lived on Colonel Childs's plantation, led a club of sixteen Red Shirts. The evidence on Washington, Taylor and Weeks, who all testified on the same day, almost one after the other, strongly suggested that they were in the same club.

b. 1: 958-962 (Green).

c. 1: 938-940 (Henderson).

d. 2: 211-214; 367-370 (Lomax).

e. 1: 962-970 (Mitchell).

f. 1: 555-556 (Taylor). Recruited by Washington, Taylor worked with him as a Democrat. Apparently Taylor also lived on Colonel Childs's plantation. He was there on election day and the blacks on "the whole plantation" ("that neighborhood") knew he was a Democrat. Therefore, he was in Washington's club.

g. 1: 560-562 (Weeks). Weeks, like Washington, belonged to Hampton before the war; both lived on Colonel Childs's plantation. As a staunch Democrat, Weeks would be a member of Washington's club. Both said they would die for Hampton.

3. Bryan Lee Dilts, comp., *1860 South Carolina Census Index* (Salt Lake City, Utah: Index Publishing, 1985), 1: 193, listed three Robert Clowneys, all from Winnsboro, Fairfield County. Brown took "Clowney" as his middle name after his employer Robert Clowney.

4. 1870 MSS Census, Population Schedules (Microfilm Series M593), National Archives, Washington, D.C.

a. George Fleming in the household of William and Hannah Fleming, Cross Hill P.O., Cross Hill Township, Laurens Co., SC, Dwelling No. 165, Family No. 165, p. 11 (Roll 1501). The census taker mistakenly listed "George" and "Leon" as females. Probably the census taker also forgot to check the "cannot read," "cannot write" and "attending school" columns for the household. No one under ten years of age was listed as attending school within the census year. Thus, it could not be assumed that George Fleming, age ten, was literate.

b. Nicholas A. Peay, Winnsboro P.O., Township No. 3, Fairfield Co., SC, Dwelling No. 121, Family No. 121, p. 102 (Roll 1496). Peay was probably Adamson's master.

c. Joseph O'Bannon, Barnwell Post Office, Barnwell Township, Barnwell Co., SC, Dwelling No. 214, Family No. 214, p. 90 (Roll 1483).

d. Jonus Weeks, Columbia P.O., Township No. 4, Richland Co., SC, Dwelling No. 1362, Family No. 1475, p. 246 (Roll 1507).

e. Aaron Mitchell, Abbeville P.O., Abbeville Township, Abbeville Co., SC, Dwelling No. 57, Family No. 62, p. 4 (Roll 1481). Census taker indicated that Mitchell could read but not write. In his household were a forty-five year old black woman named Frances, who kept house, and Ann, a twelve-year old black girl who stayed at home. Both were born in South Carolina; both could neither read nor write.

5. 1880 MSS Census, Population Schedules (Microfilm Series T9), National Archives, Washington, D.C.

a. Frank Adamson, Township No. 5, Fairfield Co., SC, Dwelling No. 158, Family No. 163, p. 136 (Roll 1229).

b. Ed Barber, Township No. 5, Fairfield Co., SC, Dwelling No. 84, Family No. 80, p. 132 (Roll 1229).

c. Andrew Brice, Township No. 2, Fairfield Co., SC, Family No. 145, p. 56 (Roll No. 1229).

d. Tom Lomax, Long Cane Township, Abbeville Co., SC, Dwelling No. 4, Family No. 4, p. 400 (Roll 1217).

e. Merimon Washington, Lower Township, Richland Co., SC, Dwelling No. 640, Family No. 672, p. 361 (Roll 1238).

f. Madison Griffin, Cromers Township No. 4, Newberry Co., SC, Dwelling No. 330, Family No. 339, p. 99 (Roll 1236).

g. Jonas Weeks, Lower Township, Richland Co., SC, Dwelling No. 648, Family No. 679, p. 362 (Roll 1238).

h. Edward Henderson, Abbeville, Abbeville Co., SC, Dwelling No. 33, Family No. 53, p. 3 (Roll 1217).

i. Asbury Green, Cokesbury Township, Abbeville Co., SC, Dwelling No. 317, Family No. 341, p. 271 (Roll 1217).

6. Newspapers.

a. Abbeville *Medium.*

1. September 13, 1876. Democratic Chairman of Abbeville County, J. S. Cothran, declared, "Let every colored Democrat have a place in the mounted procession."

2. September 20, 1876 (Mitchell).

3. October 18, 1876 (Lomax). Described the yellow uniforms of the Lowndesville club and stated, "They ride good stock."

4. October 4, 1876 (Henderson). Also mentioned that the Lowndesville club wore "bright yellow jackets."

b. Columbia *Daily Union-Herald,* October 21, 1876. Mentioned black Democrats in yellow or blue shirts at an Abbeville rally.

c. Columbia *State,* September 24, 28, 1911 (O'Bannon).

d. Abbeville *Press and Banner,* March 3, April 28, 1871 (Mitchell).

7. Miscellaneous.

a. Lowry Ware, *Old Abbeville: Scenes of the Past of a Town Where Old Time Things Are Not Forgotten* (Columbia, S.C.: SCMAR, 1992), 39 (Henderson). Abbeville black Democrats wore blue shirts.

b. Alfred B. Williams, *Hampton and His Red Shirts: South Carolina's Deliverance in 1876* (Charleston, S.C.: Walker, Evans and Cogswell, 1935), 77, identifies General John Bratton of Fairfield County. Davis rode with Bratton in 1876.

c. Julian Stevenson Bolick, *A Fairfield Sketchbook* (Clinton, S.C.: Jacobs Bros., c. 1963), 43 (Adamson); 84, 86 (Campbell). Masters and employers of Adamson and Campbell are identified.

d. Claude Henry Neuffer, ed., *Names in South Carolina* 30 (Winter 1983): 35 (Brown). Dawkins is in Fairfield County.

e. Joe Madison King, *A History of South Carolina Baptists* (Columbia: General Board of the South Carolina Baptist Convention, R. L. Bryan Co., 1964), plate VII, identifies Lower Fairforest Baptist Church in Union, Union County, S.C. Eubanks and Jones attended Red Shirt club meetings there.

f. Workers of the Writers' Program of the Work Projects Administration in the State of South Carolina, comp., *Palmetto Place Names* (Columbia: South Carolina Education Association, 1941; Reprint, Spartanburg, S.C.: Reprint Co., 1975), 53, 119; *South Carolina: The WPA Guide to the Palmetto State* (New York: Oxford University Press, 1941; Reprint, Columbia: University of South Carolina Press, 1988), 355. Charley Barber was born near Great Falls, Chester County, S.C.

g. Larry E. Hudson, Jr., *To Have and to Hold: Slave Work and Family Life in Antebellum South Carolina* (Athens: University of Georgia Press, 1997), 6 (Mack).

SOUTH CAROLINA IN 1876

Testimonies as to the Denial of the Elective Franchise in South Carolina at the Election of 1876

South Carolina Committee
U.S. Senator Angus Cameron, Chairman (Republican, Wisconsin)
U.S. Senator Isaac P. Christiancy (Republican, Michigan)
U.S. Senator Augustus Summerfield Merrimon (Democrat, North Carolina)

Preston Taylor—Richland County.

[Eight years old at the outbreak of the Civil War, this black farmer resided five miles outside of the state capitol on Colonel Childs's plantation where other black Red Shirts lived with their families. These men were abused by black women for their support of Wade Hampton.]

COLUMBIA, S.C., *December* 28, 1876.

PRESTON TAYLOR (colored) sworn and examined.

By Mr. MERRIMON:

Question. Where do you live?—Answer. In Richland County.

Q. What is your business?—A. Farming.

Q. How old are you?—A. Twenty-three.

Q. Where were you on the day of the election?—A. Right on Colonel Child's plantation.

Q. What political party do you belong to?—A. The democrats.

Q. Were you forced to join that party, or did you join it of your own free will?—A. I joined it of my own free will.

Q. State whether at any time, any of your own race, men or women, abused you for voting the democratic ticket.—A. No one didn't abuse me more than when I was coming from the polls, I said, "Hurrah for Hampton!" and the women jumped on me and tore off all my clothes; just stripped me and tore off all my clothes.

Q. Where was that?—A. Right at the box where the voting was.

By Mr. CHRISTIANCY:

Q. They left you naked?—A. Yes, sir, I was. They didn't hurt me at all, but just tore all my clothes off.

By Mr. CAMERON:

Q. When did you join the democratic party?—A. I joined in July.

Q. Who asked you to join it?—A. There wasn't no one; no one asked me to join the democratic party.

Q. Who talked to you about joining it?—A. That young fellow that was in here a while ago, (Merriman Washington.) He said to me, "I think, Pres, I will vote the democratic ticket this election." Well, I said I would do it too, if he did, and I then went to work with him. Me and him worked together.

Q. Nobody abused you?—A. Nobody, not a soul, except the women; no more than the women tearing all my clothes off of me, but none of the men even abused me at all.

Q. The colored men in that neighborhood knew that you were a democrat?—A. Yes, sir; the whole plantation.

Q. And none of them ever said a word to you about it?—A. No, sir; that is a fact.

By Mr. CHRISTIANCY:

Q. That was after you voted?—A. Yes, sir; the women done tore my clothes off after I had voted.

Jonas Weeks—Richland County.

[This black farmer also lived on Colonel Childs's plantation in Richland County. Taken to Mississippi as an infant by his master, Wade Hampton's father, Weeks was about sixteen years old when he returned to the Columbia area at the outbreak of the Civil War. Opposed by his wife, Weeks remained loyal to Hampton.]

Columbia, S.C., *December* 28, 1876.

Jonas Weeks (colored) sworn and examined.

By Mr. Merrimon:

Question. Where do you live?—Answer. Colonel Childs's plantation, five miles from town.

Q. What do you do?—A. I am a farmer.

Q. How old are you?—A. Thirty years old.

Q. To what party do you belong?—A. To the democratic party.

Q. Were you forced to go to the democratic party, or did you go with it of your own free will and pleasure?—A. I went by my own knowledge; nobody didn't persuade me.

Q. Were you ever asked by republicans if you were a democrat? If, so, state all about it.—A. Yes, sir; one of the republican men requested me to know if I was a democrat. I told him if I was dead I didn't care, I would own it anyhow. Then he called me a damned rascal, and I told him I wasn't any more a damned rascal than he was. Then he throwed a bottle at me, and I dodged the bottle. Then I picked him up and throwed him down.

Q. Who did that?—A. A republican man by the name of Ranty Thompson.

By Mr. Christiancy:

Q. A colored man?—A. Yes, sir.

By Mr. Merrimon:

Q. Did the women abuse you for being a democrat?—A. O, yes, sir; before that they did every day. They called me all kinds of names, and they would pull off my breeches and call me a devil. I told them I didn't fear any one of them by herself, but take me double at a time they could get the advantage of me and do what they chose, and I told them if I died I would die for General Hampton.

Q. What did they say about Chamberlain sending troops down there to whip you in?—A. They said that Governor Chamberlain was going to send soldiers down here to drive us off from about there.

By Mr. Christiancy:

Q. Who told you that?—A. The women said that, and a heap of the men, and they said they would run us out of the State altogether. I told them that couldn't be done, because we lived in this State, and everything that had been done in this State, should it be republican or democrat, whosoever governed, we had to go by the law, and at the same time I would support General Hampton, whether he was elected or not.

Q. Did you know General Hampton personally?—A. I used to belong to him.

Q. Do you know what a democrat is?—[A.] I think this much about it. I have been working with them ever since I was born. I belonged to General Hampton until reconstruction. I worked, and all the wages I have been working for I have got from the democratic.

Q. What democrat do you work for?—A. I worked for Mr. William Spragsen for three years, and after I quit him I worked for Bob McCullough.

Q. Whom did you work for last summer?—A. I worked for a colored man. He hired me, but I didn't got anything.

Q. Tell me, now, what is a democrat?—A. Well, I believe that it is this kind of a man: It is them that held slaves. That is what they call a democrat. They call me a democrat, too, but at the same time I don't hold slaves and never did hold any slaves; but whatsoever they call a democratic party, I says, "Well, I am a democrat; I don't care. I wasn't going to vote the republican ticket no more." I have a wife and two children, and she cussed me; and I had on a dirty shirt and she wouldn't give me no clean shirt to put on.

By Mr. Cameron:

Q. Your wife is a republican?—A. Yes, sir; she claims to be a republican, and all of them does; but I said she wasn't true to me because I supported General Hampton.

By Mr. Christiancy:

Q. Is a democrat one who supports General Hampton?—A. Yes, sir. They say that General Hampton feeds his hands on cotton-seed; and the whole parcel of republicans down in the country say that—that he feeds his niggers on cotton-seed, because I belonged to his father sixteen years, and his father died five years before the war, and I have been in Mississippi sixteen years, and in '61, when the war commenced, I came back to Columbia.

Q. Did he take you with him over to Mississippi?—A. I was raised in Mississippi.

Q. You know that he didn't feed you on cotton-seed?—A. No, sir; he didn't feed me on cotton-seed. I couldn't have been no better treated. I know I had more to eat when I was with him than I have now. They give me only three pounds of meat and a peck of meal once a week, and of course if a man hires to another man to work for him of course the man can go to work.

Q. Who was the man who undertook to strike you with a bottle?—A. Ranty Thompson; he used to belong to Frank Hampton.

Q. The brother of General Hampton?—A. Yes, sir.

Q. When was that, and where?—A. That was the day of the election, at the polls.

Q. That was after you had voted?—A. Yes, sir; that was after I had voted.

Q. Were you both drinking at that time?—A. No, sir; I wasn't drinking. I was standing there talking with some of my democratic friends, and he asked me who I voted for, and I said straight-out democrat. I said, "Yes, just give me straight-out democrat, and every man on the ticket I want to be a democrat."

Q. Can you read?—A. No, sir; I can't read.

Q. Who gave you your ticket?—A. I got it from Mr. John Seegers.

Q. Who is he?—A. He is the gentleman that makes lager beer.

Q. A white man?—A. Yes, sir. He lives right across from Mr. Childs's place.

Q. He is a democrat?—A. Yes, sir.

By Mr. Merrimon:

Q. Is General Hampton a good man?—A. Yes, sir.

Q. He treated his slaves kindly?—A. Yes, sir.

Q. They loved him?—A. Yes, sir.

By Mr. Cameron:

Q. You would rather be a slave than a free man, would you not?—A. No; he wouldn't put me back into slavery.

Q. You would rather be a slave than a free man, would you?

The Witness. Sir!

Mr. CAMERON. You would rather be a slave than to be free, as you now are?—A. If I consider that I supported General Hampton, because I supported him—because that don't put me back into slavery—I will have to abide by the law.

Q. You got more to eat when you were a slave than you do now?—Q. [A.] Yes, sir.

Q. Now, I ask you again, if you would not rather be a slave than to be free, as you now are?—A. Well, I am free in one sense; of course I am free; but at the same time if a man is free, you know you have to run your hand in your own pocket, and you have got to pay your own doctor's bills; and General Hampton pays for his and I pay for mine.

Q. But you would rather be a slave, as you were before emancipation, wouldn't you?—A. Yes, sir; if it is so fixed I had to be a slave, I would rather be a slave.

Merriman Washington—Richland County.

[A youth of twelve when the Civil War began, this black farm laborer, raised by Wade Hampton, had spent most of his life on Colonel Childs's plantation. Resentful of Republican trial justices, he switched affiliation to the Democrats and organized a black Red Shirt club with sixteen members.]

COLUMBIA, S.C., *December* 28, 1876.

MERRIMAN WASHINGTON (colored) sworn and examined.

By Mr. MERRIMON:

Question. Where do you live, and what is your business?—Answer. I live over five miles from Columbia, in Richland County, on Colonel Childs's plantation.

Q. How old are you?—A. This coming February, if I live to see the 18th, I will be twenty-eight.

Q. What political party do you belong to?—A. I belong to the democratic party.

Q. Where were you on the day of the election?—A. Down at Colonel Childs's plantation.

Q. Were you forced to join the democratic party, or did you join it of your own will?—A. I joined it of my own will, sir.

Q. Have any of the radicals of your own color abused you for being a democrat?—A. Yes, sir; they have abused me to everything they could think of.

Q. What did they say and do to you?—A. They told me if I voted for Hampton that Chamberlain was going to send United States troops down there and to shoot us all down that voted for Hampton. I told them that Chamberlain was welcome to do it, but I didn't think he would be governor.

By Mr. CAMERON:

Q. Give us the names of the persons who told you that.—A. Abram Carter, Joe Andrews, and one Cyrus Burns.

By Mr. MERRIMON:

Q. Did any women do anything to you?—A. No, sir, they didn't do anything to me, but they stripped some of my boys of their red shirts at the polls. I had a club of about sixteen head of boys, and they were to vote with me. That morning they went to the polls, and a heap of the republicans went to gasing around them and scared our boys that were there so that only eight of them voted.

By Mr. CHRISTIANCY:

Q. Who scared them?—A. The republicans.

Q. The women?—A. Yes, sir; the womens and the mens too. Nash was there with some of his crowd, and told them that his ticket was the ticket that the Lord lived on, and that they must go on his side. I told them that I didn't have any use for no republicans; that they were the damndest thieves in the world; that they had done swindled me out of $75, and that I didn't want no more of them, and that I was going to try to make it better by voting for Hampton for governor.

Q. Who did you say cheated you out of $75?—A. That was the trial-justice. It is so bad that they will swindle a man out of his money and throw him out of the street. You can't speak, but you are seized and brought before some trial-justice, and they will cheat you out of everything you have got. That is the reason I want the other governor, so that we can break up the trial-justices. I don't want no more of them.

By Mr. MERRIMON:

Q. Do you know of any colored democrats being tied by the women and thrown in the creek?—A. I didn't see that with my own eyes.

Q. Explain anything you may know about the colored democrats who came from Trenholm's to Big Lake to vote the democratic ticket.—A. They came up there, and when they met me in a company of them, a great many of them was in my company; they had a wagon, and I hurrahed for Hampton; and I told them to "Come on, boys, and let us go to the polls, and if we all die, let us die;" and we went to the polls, and when we got there a republican party formed in line about what is called four deep, right across the way of coming up to the polls; and they had so many more than we had that they kept our men off.

By Mr. CHRISTIANCY:

Q. What poll was that?—A. Down at Trenholm's precinct.

Q. Is that where you voted?—A. Yes, sir. They wouldn't let them vote. They would jump on them, and knock them down, and tear all their clothes off; and we would have had a terrible time, but Willie Childs was there, and he run in there and got a hold of me by the arm, and McDuff, and said, "You must not make any row; if they want to fight you, you let them, because if we raise any row they will have us dead, and we will lose three hundred or four hundred votes."

By Mr. MERRIMON:

Q. Were any of those men scared off from the polls?—A. Yes, sir; about fifteen of them was scared off, so that they didn't vote at all.

By Mr. CHRISTIANCY:

Q. Who were these that were scared off?

The WITNESS. Who are they?

Mr. CHRISTIANCY. Yes.

A. I can't tell you all; I can tell you some of them. Tom Simmons was one and a fellow named Squire Mack, and I can't think of all the boys: and one named Frank Corbins, they scared him off.

Q. Did any of the men tell you that they wanted to vote the democratic ticket?—A. Yes, sir; they told me certainly they would do it. If I voted it, they would all vote the same ticket that I voted, or else they would die right at the polls.

Q. Did any of the radicals say anything to you about United States troops being sent down there to intimidate the democratic colored club?—A. Yes, sir.

Q. What did they say?—A. They said Chamberlain had United States troops to come here to the election, and to be right at the polls and take down every nigger that voted for Hampton—to take his name down on a piece of paper—and as soon as the election was over the soldiers were going to shoot the negro democrats and the white democrats. I told them I would be willing to die with Hampton any day. Hampton raised me, and I know that he wasn't a coward, and I ain't a coward.

By Mr. CAMERON:

Q. Were you ever taken up and taken before any of these trial-justices?

The WITNESS. Was I taken up?

Mr. CAMERON: Yes.

By Mr. CHRISTIANCY:

Q. Were you charged with any offense?—A. No, sir; yes, I was. I had to come up here before a trial-justice about Phil. Grandison. They had to take Phil. Grandison and put him in prison because he was going to join the democratic party. Him and a colored man named Gen. Hames had some dispute, and he come up to town and had him arrested before Thompson, and had him put in jail, and I come up here next day to get him out.

By Mr. CAMERON:

Q. You said that these trial-justices had cheated you out of $75?—A. O, yes, sir; they swindled me out of that before this election.

Q. Who did that?—A. This here Thompson and a white man named Mr. Sills.

Q. How did they swindle you out of it?—A. Just like this gentleman would be here and you would be talking, and I would come up there and I would ask you whether you wanted me to go in or not, and would just listen to the argument, and I would say a word in there and you would tell me to stop and I wouldn't stop.

By Mr. CHRISTIANCY:

Q. You need not suppose a case; tel[l] what happened to you.—A. They had me brought there for fighting, before these trial-justices.

Q. They had you taken there for fighting?—A. Yes, sir.

By Mr. CAMERON:

Q. You had a fight?—A. O, yes, sir; long before the election.

Q. You were arrested and taken before a trial-justice for that?—A. Yes, sir.

Q. How much were you fined?—A. I was fined $16.75, and I had to pay that or else go to jail, and I paid it.

By Mr. CHRISTIANCY:

Q. That don't make $75.—A. No, sir; but they sued me four times before these trial-justices. Mr. Thompson sued me twice for fighting, and Mr. Coleman once, and this here Mr. Sills, and the whole was four times, and it come to $75.

By Mr. CAMERON:

Q. And you were sued for fighting?—A. Yes, sir.

Q. Did you fight each time?—A. Yes, sir; I did do it.

Q. That is why you left the republican party?—A. Yes, sir.

Q. Whose land do you live on?—A. I lives on Col. Childs' plantation.

Q. How long have you lived there?—A. I have lived there all my life-time but seven years. This coming February I will be twenty-eight years, and I have never been off the place more than seven years. You can tell how long I have been staying there.

Q. Childs is a democrat, is he not?—A. Yes, sir.

Q. And you work a part of his land?—A. Yes, sir.

Q. How much do you work?—A. Well, they don't measure land here at all. The owner charges us $40 to a door. All the houses that have doors on them, and every man stays in his house, and I don't care if he has two mules, he hardly ever pays more than $40.

Q. When did you join the democratic party?

The WITNESS. When did I join?

Mr. CAMERON. Yes; at what time did you go into the democratic party?

The WITNESS. What time did I vote?

Mr. CAMERON. No, no; what time did you leave the republicans and go over to the democrats?—A. This same year.

Q. This year?—A. Yes, sir.

Q. After Hampton was inaugurated for governor, or before?—A. O, before, long before that; nearly August, I believe, it was.

Q. That was before Hampton was nominated?—A. O, yes, sir.

Q. About what time was he nominated, do you remember?—A. No, sir; I don't remember.

Q. But you do remember that you left the republican party in August?—A. Yes, sir.

Q. And that was before Hampton was nominated?—A. Yes, sir.

Q. You are sure of that, are you?—A. I am sure that he was not nominated for governor then.

Edward Henderson—Abbeville County.

[Born in 1828 to a slave woman and a white lawyer, this fair-skinned carpenter was related to one of South Carolina's prominent families, the Laurens. Although illiterate, he was an effective Democratic canvasser and headed a Democratic club of 180 members. His wife and daughter as well as he were vilified by black Republicans.]

COLUMBIA, S.C., *December* 29, 1876.

EDWARD HENDERSON (colored) sworn and examined.

By Mr. MERRIMON:

Question. State your place of residence and your business.—Answer. Abbeville; a carpenter.

Q. To what political party do you belong?—A. To the democratic.

Q. State whether you took any part in the late political canvass in this State; and, if you say yes, state what it was.—A. I did.

Q. Give us an account now of your experiences during the campaign.—A. I went around and quietly requested the colored people to go with the democratic party.

Q. Were you, at the time, president of a colored club?—A. Yes, sir.

Q. At what point?—A. Abbeville.

Q. How many members were in it?—A. About 180.

Q. Did you make any speeches?—A. A very few.

Q. Did you observe any demonstrations of violence anywhere toward anybody? and if you say yes, state when and where.—A. Nary one.

Q. State whether or not, at any time, you were attacked; and, if so, by whom.—A. Yes, sir.

Q. By whom?—A. Mr. Bruce, trial-justice there, attacked me.

Q. Is he a white man?—A. Yes, sir.

Q. What else was he besides a trial-justice?—A. United States marshal. I think there was two workmen that worked with me came down to the meeting in the school-house and joined the club, and there was about forty or fifty of his men, and they came and attended the club, and he got angry about it.

Q. What did he say to you about it?—A. We got into a dispute about it, and I told him that I had used only fair arguments with these men, and he said I hadn't, and I told him I hadn't done anything out of the way, and he said I had; and he was drinking then, and treating a great many, and spending his money in that way, and I told him that I didn't use any money nor no violence. Then he called me a liar, and attempted to draw his pistol out, but he didn't shoot; but he said he would do it in case it was necessary.

And the colored women was the worst of all. I have been rebuked a good deal by them through the county—at Lowndesville, at Greenville, and Calhoun's Mills. They were there at the meetings.

Q. What did they do?—A. They abused me, and all the men that were with me. They whipped several. We had a big dinner down there, and some speeches.

By Mr. Christiancy:

Q. Did they attack anybody but colored men?—A. No, sir, I think not.

Q. You are not a colored man, are you?—A. Yes, sir.

By Mr. Merrimon:

Q. You say the women abused you violently?—A. O, tremendously. They whipped my little girl at the school, and threatened to whip my wife at church.

By Mr. Cameron:

Q. Did you hear that yourself?—A. I saw it. The parties were arrested for whipping my girl; and I was going home to dinner one day, and they were after my wife, coming from the spring, and they called her bad names, "a dirty bitch," &c.; and when they saw me coming they left. There was several men that wanted to join my club that couldn't do it on account of the women portion of the family. But they did vote, some of them, the democratic ticket, I believe. I don't know who did or who didn't.

Q. Do you know any argument the women resorted to to keep the men from voting the democratic ticket?—A. Yes, sir; some smutty things.

Q. Well, go on and state them.—A. Well, they would say that they were not going to support their husbands; that they would starve them; and that they wouldn't sleep in the same bed with them. And I knew one woman in town that threw her husband's clothes out the door and locked the door on him, and he went back and got to drinking some, and he came over to my house and asked me to go home with him, and I went there with him, and I knocked on the door of his house, and there happened to be another man jumped out of the window and left, and she let him in, and then they staid quiet a day or two. And the day of the election I don't think he voted, but I never could find out. There was another man there, that lived with General McGowan, a nice man, about forty-five years old. He was a bright-looking man, and he wanted to vote the democratic ticket, and he wanted to vote for General McGowan, because he lived with him; and his wife whipped him in the street, took his hat, and torn his coat off, and took him up by the school-house, to make him vote the republican ticket, and I don't think he voted at all.

By Mr. Christiancy:

Q. Do you think he deceived his wife and made her think he voted the republican ticket?—A. He did.

By Mr. Merrimon:

Q. Did you know any cases where they refused to sleep with their husbands?—A. Yes, sir; this same woman that had run her husband off and had this colored man there with her, she said she wouldn't have any democratic nigger sleep with her as long as she lived, and she would beg her bread first. And they are now separated, and this other colored man has taken her and carried her to Greenville.

Q. State anything you saw in the way of intimidation or abuse on account of color or political affiliation on either side.—A. I saw nothing on the day of the election at Abbeville. If there was anything I didn't see it. I didn't see a pistol except what was with the republican party, not one. There was a meeting there two days before to prevent it, and we went up there and we all pledged ourselves not to use any violence, and I didn't see no pistols there on that day, except what was with the republican party. Mr. Guffin brought in a company, I think, of about two hundred from a box in the country where something went wrong and they couldn't vote; they come in with clubs and pistols, and I reckon about a dozen shot-guns.

Q. Did they march them in military order?—A. Yes, sir; regular two deep. The drove was over half a mile long.

Q. Armed men?—A. There was some armed and some were not.

Q. Did you use any force to induce the colored people to vote the democratic ticket?—A. Not one word; I never had a cross word with a man in the campaign, with the exception of Mr. Bruce, the man I have mentioned, and he was—I think William Pope, down there, will give me credit that I acted more gentlemanly than any man he knew there. He was on the election there and treated me handsomely, and Griffin did the same.

Q. Do you know any other fact that you ought to state here in the line of the examination I have given you?—A. No, sir.

CROSS-EXAMINATION.

By Mr. CAMERON:

Q. When did you join the democratic party?—A. I have always been a democrat. The first election we ever had at Abbeville I had a club of one hundred and seven.

Q. One hundred and seven colored men?—A. Yes, sir.

Q. In what year?—A. That was in 1867, I believe, sir, as well as I remember.

Q. You have been a democrat ever since?—A. Yes, sir.

Q. By whom are you principally employed as a carpenter, by republicans or democrats?—A. I get employment from both.

Q. I supposed that; but by whom are you principally employed?—A. Principally by the democrats, because they have more work. I have done a good deal of work for Guffin; I had over two hundred dollars' worth of work.

Q. You are employed principally by the democrats?—A. Yes, sir.

Q. They have the most work to do?—A. Yes, sir; the republicans have not done much around there. I have worked a good deal for the colored people around there. I think I have made over fifty coffins for the colored people in the last two years, and I don't believe I have got two dollars for it.

Q. The colored people of Abbeville are generally poor, are they not?—A. Well, yes, sir; generally poor.

Q. Were you a slave before the war?—A. Yes, sir.

Q. Who was your owner?—A. John McLaren.

Q. Does he reside at Abbeville still?—A. He is dead. I was raised by him.

Asbury Green—Abbeville County.

[A twelve-year-old slave at the outbreak of the Civil War, this sharecropper had increasing difficulty supporting his wife and five children during Reconstruction. By switching to the Democratic Party and wearing the red shirt, he hoped to get good government and wages. The female members of his church prevented him from attending services.]

COLUMBIA, S.C., *December* 29, 1876.

ASBURY GREEN (colored) sworn and examined.

By Mr. MERRIMON:

Question. How old are you?—Answer. I am twenty-seven years old, I think, as near as I can come at my age.

Q. Where do you live?—A. At Hodge's Depot, Abbeville.

Q. What is your business?—A. Farmer.

Q. What political party do you belong to?—A. Well, I used to belong to the radical party, but I changed. I concluded I would join the democratic club.

Q. Where?—A. For one reason why I changed, every year I was working hard, and the harder I worked the worser I got, and I just said, "I will try another party now this year, and see if we can't all have a good government, white and black, and have money a plenty, and get good wages and paid for our labor," and so on.

Q. Where was that; where did your club meet?—A. It met at Hodge's Depot.

Q. How many colored men went with you?—A. Well, sir, there was somewhere about twenty-five or thirty, maybe a little more than that.

Q. Did anybody force you to go that way?—A. O, no, sir; no one didn't force me at all.

Q. You went that way of your own will?—A. I did; I was twenty-one [twenty-seven], and I just took it in my head. I said the way I was working with my family, I could not support them. The rations were high, and everything was high, and I said, "I will have to try another party—this of ours is swindling me—and see if they will make it no better, and if they don't I don't know what in the world to do."

We came down to the polls of a Monday night, before Tuesday, the day of the election, that we might be there all night and get up to the polls as soon as anybody and vote and get out of the way. We got breakfast a little while before day; I could not exactly say what time they ate; and then they all marched out two by two, locked arms, up to the polls. It was not so powerful long before day opened, and we walked up and voted, and by the time we got done voting Beverly Vance marched up there with his crowd, and he says, "Well, men, as soon as you get through, fall back and let us get in;" and I says, "As soon as we get through of course we will get out of the way."

Well, we got out of the way, and the boys says, "Well, now we got Hampton at the bottom, now we'll ram Chamberlain on top and kill him dead," jes so. He says, "Now, we'll ram Chamberlain right in and kill Hampton dead, and keep him at the bottom, and we'll hold him there; and I have got about seventy-five or a hundred coming up here." They were all armed with great clubs. I said to him, "What do you colored men all want of clubs? We ain't got no clubs." We just marched up two by two with the white men when we voted, and no swearing and nothing of the sort, and I never saw such a peaceful elect[i]on in all my life.

Q. You were not afraid of them?—A. No, sir.

Q. Were you treated with violence?—A. None at all.

Q. Did you see any men with pistols on?—A. None at all. I was there all day. I just staid there, I reckon, about half an hour, and some gentleman sent me up to town on horseback to bring a few ground-peas down there to sell there that day; and white men bought, and colored men bought, and we had the best time, and Mr. Guffin said it himself. He said we had the best time that he ever saw in his life. I think it was Will Guffin, and he said, "Why, a man might spit on me"—you know how fine he talks—"a man might spit in my face, before I would raise a row here to-day;" and they all just laughed like—you know, and some like them sung those funny songs, you know, to keep up the fun.

Q. You had a jolly time there that day?—A. O, yes, sir; we had fun.

By Mr. CAMERON:

Q. Could you not sing us one of your songs now?—A. I know one they sung.

Q. Give us a stanza from one of the songs.—A. They sung this. (Witness sings to the tune of John Brown:)

> "We'll hang Lem Guffin on a hickory tree,
> We'll hang Lem Guffin on a hickory tree,
> We'll hang Lem Guffin on a hickory tree,
> As we go marching along.
>   Glory, glory, hallelujah!
>   Glory, glory, hallelujah!
>   As we go marching along."

Just that way; sung that, you know, to keep up the fun. Some of them had been up all night, and we sung that to be lively; and my whole color just turned out, and all the men that joined the democratic club went up with me and voted.

Q. Did any of them ever abuse you?—A. Good gracious alive, if abusing would kill me I would have been dead long ago. But I didn't pay no attention to it at all. Me and my daughter and another girl that was staying with me, they wanted to go to a party, and I says, "I don't want to go." And she said, "Let's go;" and I said, "Let's not go, for they will get into a row and abuse me." And she said, "I reckon not," and so prevailed upon me to go; and when I went, the first man I approached, he says, "You God damned democrat, I have a good mind to just pull my pistol out and shoot you." I didn't pay no attention; I was just going by myself; I wanted to be peaceable. There was one man, he says to me, "You damned democrat nigger, you can't come in my house for nothing. If you do I will kick you out." I says, "From all accounts I don't spect you will have any house very long, because I know you haven't paid for no house, and when your year is up, if you don't do right you will have to leave." Says I, "I am twenty one, and I am going to vote the democratic ticket anyhow; and I think that I feel it my duty to do so; and if I can't support my family the way I am going on, I want a change in the government. I never have got no good out of the republican party. I never have got ten cents out of the party."

Q. How were the women?—A. The women? Why, they were just like a rattlesnake; why, they didn't allow me to go to my church. I would pull out the money on Sunday, when they went around with the 'lection, to get money enough to buy a good church—I would say, "Good evening, gentlemen; Good morning, ladies; how do you all do?" and they would pay no attention to me at all; and I says, "Well, I won't go to that church any more; and if they get any more money out of me, they will have to steal it;" and I says, "What money I make hereafter, I will put it on my family"—jes so. And I didn't support that church no more. They 'buked me because I voted with the white people; and now look at them—they ain't got a piece of bread hardly in the house.

Q. Is that all you know about it?—A. Well, I believe that's about the principal part of what I have to say on the subject.

CROSS-EXAMINATION.

By Mr. CAMERON:

Q. Did you make any speeches?—A. No, I didn't make no speeches at all.

Q. What did you do to persuade the negroes to vote the democratic ticket?—A. I didn't do nothing only I just went with them with our club to the speeches.

Q. How many democratic speeches did you attend?—A. Well, let me see; I was at four or five, I think; according to my recollection.

Q. Did you wear a red shirt?—A. Yes, sir.

Q. Did you ride on horseback?—A. Yes, sir.

Q. Who paid for your red shirt?—A. It was bought and give to me, I reckon. It was give to me.

Q. The white people gave it to you?—A. Yes, sir.

Q. Did the white people furnish you a horse to ride when you went?—A. Yes, sir; and I took that course because I wanted to get a good government.

Q. You thought by putting on a red shirt and riding a good horse to the democratic meeting you would get a good government, did you?—A. I really wanted a good government. I took the red shirt just because they gave it to me, not because I was keen towards it; and when they gave me a horse to ride on I thought I would take it. I knowed the red shirt would be good for cold weather.

Q. You thought the red shirt would help keep you warm, didn't you?—A. Yes, sir; it would help to keep me warm, sir.

Q. You liked a red shirt and a horse to ride on, did you not?—A. Sometimes.

Q. Well, your red shirt did not cost you anything?—A. No, my red shirt didn't cost me anything.

Q. Your horse did not cost you anything, did it?—A. No, sir; it didn't cost me nothing.

Q. Did any of the colored people beat you, or whip you, or strike you because you were a democrat?—A. No, sir; they didn't do that, but they came so near it that I thought they would get up a disturbance. They threatened me just enough, and I just stood out agin them, you know; I wouldn't let them scare me; I just wouldn't be put down by them, but I would always keep out of the way of making a fuss or raising a row with them.

Q. Did the women whip you or beat you?—A. The women?

Q. Yes.—A. Why, they insulted me, and they persuaded with my wife to quit me, because I voted the democratic ticket; and five living children in the family.

Q. Your wife wouldn't do it?—A. She wouldn't do it. She knowed I was the only one to take care of her.

Q. Were you a slave before the war?—A. O, yes, sir.

Q. Who was your master?—A. A man by the name of Juicy Bill Bucannan.

Q. Where does he live now?—A. He lives, I think, six miles from the Dead Falls Bridge, up above Greenwood, between Abbeville and Hodges, from that down on the old Abbeville road to the court house.

Q. From whom did you rent land this year?—A. I didn't rent none at all; I was farming with a white man who lived two miles and a half above Hodges Depot.

Q. You worked by the day, did you?—A. I farmed for myself. He furnished me with tools and I farmed for myself, with my own team, and he gave me a part of the crop.

Q. Is he a democrat?—A. O, yes, sir.

Q. What is his name?—A. William Martin. His father—his name is Yancey Martin.

Q. I think you said that there were a good many colored people there who voted the republican ticket who have not got a piece of bread in the houses now?—A. Yes, sir; there's some of them.

Q. They are very poor?—A. Yes, sir.

Q. You told them when they spoke about putting you out of the house that they would not have any house very long, did you?—A. I told them that because they called me a democrat.

Q. You told them that they wouldn't have a house?—A. I told them that to try and match them.

Q. Well, it is true that you did wear a red shirt?—A. Yes, sir; I didn't try to hide it.

Q. You thought it was true that they would not have any house very long, did you not?—A. Yes, sir; it did look like it sure enough.

Q. You told them that if they didn't do right they would not have any house at all?—A. No, sir; I didn't pursuade [persuade] them at all. Didn't do nothing of the sort; I just said it in that way—just like they would.

Q. What have you done with that red shirt?—A. I got it on underneath now.

Q. You have it on now?—A. Yes, sir.

Q. A very good thing to have, is it not?—A. It keeps me warm.

Q. Have you had plenty of money since you voted the democratic ticket? —A. Well, I ain't had plenty, but every time I went for it I always got it.

Q. Every time you called upon your democratic friends for money they let you have it?—A. Yes, sir.

Q. Well, I believe they let republicans have it, too, when they call for it? —A. O, yes, sir.

Q. Whenever any democratic negro calls upon any white man for money he gives them all they want, does he?—A. I don't carry it so far as that; I never called for any but a few times, because I didn't want to say that I had joined their party and straightway had begun to beg of them. I didn't want to have them say that.

Q. How much money have you got from white men since the election? —A. I have got from ten to twelve dollars.

Q. Have you paid it back yet?—A. No, sir. They give it to me.

Q. You do not expect to pay it back?—A. They didn't ask me to pay it back.

Q. Do you still live on the land with that man Martin?—A. Yes, sir.

Q. Have you taken a contract for next year?—A. Not yet.

Q. When do you expect to take a contract for next year?—A. Just as soon as Christmas goes out.

Q. You are pretty sure he will give you a contract for next year, are you?—A. Well, he says that he will give me a showin'. I have been there for four years, and he says that he will give me a showin', and he would do as well by me as I could do anywhere else. I have been there a long time, and I have cleaned up the land for him a good deal, and I said before I would move on to anybody else's land I would stay on the place just as long as ever I could.

Q. Were you not better off when you were a slave than you have been since you have been free?—A. No, sir; I do not consider that I am any better off—any real better off—but I tries to live and let live. Don't try to take nothing from nobody, and I tries to make my living.

Q. Were you a pretty active republican until this fall?

WITNESS. Me?

Q. Yes.—A. O, no, sir. I never voted the democratic ticket but this last coming year; I have always been radical.

Q. You used to vote the radical ticket?—A. Yes, sir.

Q. Were you a pretty active republican? Did you work?

The WITNESS. What, sir?

Q. Did you work a good deal for the republicans?—A. O, yes, sir; I worked all the time.

Aaron Mitchell—Abbeville County.

[Born in 1816, this black Republican was a traveling blacksmith-mechanic. Fed up with local Republican corruption and incompetency, he became a Democrat. His leadership abilities are evident from his testimony.]

COLUMBIA, S.C., *December* 29, 1876.

AARON MITCHELL (colored) sworn and examined.

By Mr. MERRIMON:

Question. State your age.—Answer. I will be sixty-one in May next.

Q. What is your business?—A. Blacksmith—mechanic. Blacksmith by trade and a journey-work man.

Q. Now state where you reside?—A. I am stationed in Abbeville village.

Q. What do you mean by "stationed;" that you live there?—A. Yes, sir. Then I journey-work. I have eight shops, about thirty-two miles from the time that I leave home until I come back; traveling workman in the upper portion of the country.

Q. State what political party you belong to, and whether you took any part in the late political campaign in this State?—A. Yes, sir; I did. I belonged to the republican party from 1868 up until last June, about the first of June.

Q. What party then did you attach yourself to or co-operate with?—A. The democratic party, sir.

Q. Now go on and state the reasons why you changed your politics, your political relations, and anything that you observed during the late campaign, in your own way.—A. I had been a strong republican to—

Mr. CHRISTIANCY. I do not think that you should go into the reasons why he changed his politics.

Mr. MERRIMON. You have allowed it all along.

Mr. CHRISTIANCY. The fact that he changed it is enough.

Mr. MERRIMON. I want the Senate to see that he was not intimidated; that he had good reasons for it.

WITNESS. I had been in the republican party from 1868, and had followed it, and watched it in my own county. What has disgusted me. I looked at the incompetence of the representatives to the legislature, and the county offices which would be elected there, and I saw the abuses, and then, in other words, I looked after it for the past two years—I thought, I will be convinced; and though I could hear of some great moves, a great many of them went by, and there was no action taken, nothing at all, and I got disgusted with the party. I didn't propose to go back on the State ticket until long up in August, but the county ticket I did expect—I didn't expect to vote for a man for no county office at all, but still I kept that to myself; I didn't say anything about it; finally, as I stated, I walked in where the democrats had met, went to General McGowan who was seated at the bar and told him I wanted him to put my name down on the democrat club, and he says to me, says he, "Is that possible?" says I, "Yes." says he, "Well, all right; just go on; we are busy now." After that he called my attention to it, and asked me did I mean what I said, and I told him I did.

I went on so, and in the course of a few weeks the people began to find it out, the people that I had been staying with, sleeping with, and that account of me got circulated about, and they told me that I couldn't stay with them, that I was a democrat, and that I couldn't sleep in their house no longer, or in their bed, and I told them, said I, "That don't make any difference with me; I have a perfect right to do as I please about that["]; if they threw me out on that account I would get out of the way. On two or three of my circuits I had to stay in my shop at nights. Finally, I reported to the white people that I was working for how I was treated, and they gave me a place to sleep. Then I were disbanded from church, for they said they wanted no democrat to come into church—the church is 200 yards of my house—and my wife were treated the same.

Q. Did they turn you out?—A. They didn't turn me out then, but my leader in the class meeting he said he wouldn't notice me in the church. Well, he didn't do it, and never spoke to me since the first of September until last Sunday was a week ago. He has been my class leader in the church for five years, and the last time he spoke to me was about the first of September, I believe, and he never spoke to me until Sunday a week ago he came to me and offered me his hand. "Ain't we never going to come together?" he said. "You democrats, I ain't got no use for you, but you can come back to your class." I have not been there since the first of September at all yet. They invited me to go last Sunday was a week. My wife were treated in the same way. Well, I shuffled along the best I could. I don't know whether any of you gentlemen know of it, there was a joint discussion there. Mr. Chamberlain, Pope, and Jillson was there. It was a joint discussion; on Tuesday, I think. Some short time after that there was another one appointed, and there was a great many republicans come that evening; this was on Wednesday, the second meeting. Well, I had been off to my shops, and my attention were called in the evening to come up to the meeting. They asked me where I had been; I told them I had been around to my shops. The democratic party invited me to come up to the meeting; they said, "Well, we are going to have a dinner to-morrow, and you must come up." I went home and told my wife she must close up her business; that there was going to be a dinner to-morrow. She said she must iron all the clothes for the young men that she had got on hand. I said, "Iron what you are 'bliged to to-night, and let the rest go." I comes to town about sundown, and the republicans were abusing me, and they called me a damn democrat, and I goes off; about sunset I starts and goes home; and my wife starts to ironing as soon as she gets me a bite of supper. I heard a terrible hollering, and hooping, and yelling up the street. I live two blocks from the public square—from the court-house. They turned when they came down the cross-street where I live on.

By Mr. Christiancy:

Q. Who were those people coming down?—A. Republicans; about fifty or one hundred of them, I suppose; I didn't look out at them—I couldn't identify a man of them—until they got right to my gate, which is not wider from the front door than this room is wide; one fellow that had been going around to these meetings, Harry Calahan, he says, "Here's the damn democrat's house." He got up on the fence—my fence—which is a little shaky, and shook it; and my wife said, "They are going to tear the fence down." And I said, "I can't help it; I can't go out." They were hollering, and yelling, and cursing around there, and they finally fired one pistol. My wife was all in a tremble, and it shocked me too. I heard it hit the house. The second shot struck the plate about five feet from the eaves, and fell right down on the floor in the room where we were; and my wife said she couldn't go on with the ironing. I said, "I can't help it; you will have to quit." We sat there perfectly quiet, and I never went to the door. I waited, and [t]hey cursed, and yelled, and abused us; and they went on that way the whole night, and we slept none. I sat in a chair the whole night. My wife laid down across the bed, but she didn't sleep.

By Mr. Merrimon:

Q. Did they stay right there all night?—A. They didn't, but they passed on, then came back again—a dozen or twenty fellows; I don't know it was the same crowd, but it was republicans; I know that. I didn't say a word about it the next day, but after that the mayor of the town called my attention that he heard that my house was fired on. I told him that it was. He said, "Why didn't you report that to me?" I said, "I didn't care to do it; nobody was hurt." He said, "It must be did." It was Mr. Parker, a lawyer. I said, "I will go and see my lawyer about it," and I goes to General McGowan and talked with him about it, and he says, "There's nobody hurt, and don't let us make a bad thing of a good thing. Just let it go, if no harm has been done." I said, "No, no harm done, except a little hole shot through my house as big as my finger," and I showed him the ball.

Q. Have you got it now?—A. No, sir; I showed it to a good many persons. I taken all the rebuking, and I went around to this meeting. I did talk, and prevailed with the people, and gave them my views, and numbers have come away, after I gave them my views and gave them satisfactory, and joined with me. I couldn't tell how many. The most hardest place in the county, which is called Calhoun's Mills, I went there, and none of the colored people belonged to the democratic party. They wanted me to go down there and work among the colored people, and when they adjourned for dinner, at the meeting they had there, they wouldn't let me go to dinner; but I went to work then, and twenty-one joined right there.

By Mr. CHRISTIANCY:

Q. About what time in the year was this?—A. I don't recollect how long; it was one of the meetings that they held.

Q. Was it in October?—A. I think it was in October; I am not certain. I can't say about the date, but they all passed off friendly.

Q. On what occasion; at Calhoun's Mills?—A. Yes, sir; there was several speeches had been made. Several colored men came up to me and said, "Mr. Mitchell, will the white people allow us to come up to their meeting?" Says I, "Yes; these white men are speaking to black men as well as to white men." Says I, "Come up and hear for yourself;" and I goes to some gentlemen, and the white people gave one whole side up to the colored people and got them up to the meeting, and the colored people rushed up and heard the discussion. They hadn't been but very few standing up close until about dinner. They went down and taken dinner with us that evening at the table, when I explained myself to some gentlemen. Said I, "Let these men, if they don't join us, come up and eat," and some one spoke up and said, "O, well, we don't propose to feed them;" but I got them to let the colored people come up, and after the democrats got through they came up and eat there. The time came for me to go—I lived twelve miles from there—and I left, and I heard from there in a day or two, and they said they were doing very well up there and others had joined.

By Mr. MERRIMON:

Q. Do you remember anything further that happened before the election in the line of what you have been telling to us?—A. I know nothing at all, sir, but abusing.

Q. Do you know that many colored people voted the democratic ticket?—A. I do, sir; I voted as many as between one and two hundred at Abbeville Court-House right at one box—there was two boxes there—I am satisfied of that.

Q. Were they forced to do it?—A. No, sir; they did this: they slipped away from their wives and others, and numbers of them on account of their wives, that would have voted the democratic ticket, that were 'buked so by their wives and other women that they were feared to vote, and up to this very day there's one colored man that his wife has left him, and has not had anything to do with him in two months. Some came to me on the day of election and got tickets and slipped in and voted the democratic ticket, that I had no more idea that they were going to vote the democratic ticket than that I am sleeping now. They got me to watch them until they did vote it. Well, they had the republican ticket too, and they voted the democratic ticket.

By Mr. Christiancy:

Q. About two hundred of them that you took up at Abbeville CourtHouse, to poll No. 1, did you say?—A. Yes, sir; there was two polls there, but the second one, I wasn't up there at all. I attended at the court-room, but there was one at the school-room, about three squares from there. I did walk over there once to see how things were going there. There was very few democratic votes there. There was one there that belonged to our club who had been with us, and been all over the county, and we counted on him, but on the day of election he went right clear back on us and voted the republican ticket. He went around in the county with us and enjoyed himself with us all the time, and on the day of election he went right back on us and voted the republican ticket.

By Mr. Merrimon:

Q. You say that you traveled over the county very generally?—A. I traveled over it for nearly three weeks.

Q. Did you see any force used on the part of white people to compel the colored people to vote with them?—A. No, sir; I saw them persuaded, but I never saw any men try to compel them: not a word of it. I have been in every corner of the county and then in other places.

Q. You have seen the colored people very generally?—A. Yes, sir; and I staid with them, and I have been to thirteen meetings, sir—public meetings—during the canvass, and I was at three they didn't call public, that I was sent for and went to by myself.

Q. Did you see any demonstration or violence during the election by any of the radicals?—A. No; I didn't see any especially, but I was insulted after I made my speech, at every meeting. There was a crowd from Magnolia came in, I think, about 12 or 1 o'clock. The voting was pretty much done, and they was coming in scattering, and was standing talking and laughing there, while the female women was abusing and going on terrible. We heard a powerful hollering, seemed to be about one-half or three-fourths of a mile off. I didn't know what it meant, and after standing and looking on a while, we saw a crowd coming on the main street; one man rode in front on his horse, and there was two on each side galloping up and down. These riders, the men that were riding in front, one of them had one of these big war-swords with a brass case on it, and those that were riding up and down kept them in line, they were riding in military order, and hollering backward and forward. Well, I was standing in the court-room, and there was an old man, Robert Wordlow, he came to me and said, "Mitchell, how do you feel now; are you scared?" I said, "I am not scared."

They came along riding, and there were a great many boys in the procession—there was some voters among then, and every one had a club about that long, (indicating.) I think it was a club over two feet and a half long, and green-oak clubs, as big as my arm—just took them in their hands, not for walking-sticks at all. They passed right on until they got over to the school room, and after they had got over there pretty much, Mr. L. L. Guffin rushed down from the court-room, where he was standing at the polls, and in about twenty minutes he came back, I suppose with one hundred or one hundred and fifty, I suppose about one-half of them, he fotched [fetched] them back, him in front of them. I was standing to one side of the court-room there, and he came right on and he says, "Mitchell, get out of the way;" and I says, "Mr. Guffin, here's room enough, I am not in the way." I was standing there with my tickets in my hand. Says he, "Come on, boys" and one fellow says, "That's a damn democrat nigger, God damn him;" another one said, "Don't you offer me any of your damn democrat tickets; if you do I will knock you into hell in a minute." I said, "Pass on, gentlemen, I know you don't want my tickets." One of them says, "No, don't you offer me one; if you do I will knock you into hell."

I never offered them one; they passed on straight like bulls, and they looked so blood-thirsty I was afraid, and I got down out of the way; and some women were there, and they cried out, "There's that damn democrat nigger, knock him, knock him down, knock him to hell in a minute."

I then walks quietly off to Mr. Parker, the intendant of the town, and I says, "I will have to leave there if you don't get the marshal to get them women out of the way;" and he got the marshal to go and quiet them somewhat, and the colored men came on down again and looked at me and said, "Damn your soul, you better stay in town here, you democrat nigger. If you ever come out we will fix you." I said, "Don't abuse me about my principle, you vote as you please." Mr. Guffin says, "Go on, boys, don't say nothing to him; go home, boys, they are trying to get up something here, and make it out that some of you is voting twice." But after the election I went around to my shops again, but I can't stay among them colored people, the feeling is still so bad.

Q. State whether any violence was done to you after the election at any time?—A. Not until last Monday.

Q. What happened to you then?—A. There was a great enjoying of snow-balling on the street, everybody was enjoying themselves up there; and the white men and the black men in the town, and they were wallowing and engaged in snow-balling all in fun. Some white ladies down there got to snow-balling, and they called me to help them to make snow-balls for them, and I helped them a little while, and they whipped out the gentlemen they were snow-balling with, and the white gentlemen saw me, and said that I had caused them to whip them, and the white men took me and they gave me a wallowing. That all passed, and they took me then into the bar and treated me; and there was an old black man come along and there was some money matters between him and me. I was owing him fifty or sixty cents and he asked me for the money. I says to him, "There's no money passing to day, we are all enjoying Christmas." He says, "I have got to have that money, you infernal rogue; you want to steal my money, you damn son of a bitch." Said I, "Don't go to abusing me;" says I, "Let's enjoy Christmas;" and says he, "Look here, Mr. Mitchell, don't you come near me, or I will split your head open;" and then he came over and bled me like a hog with a large hickory stick; he struck me right here, (indicating mark on back of his head.)

I goes to Mr. Parker, and I told him that I wanted a warrant for him, and he said, "Let Christmas pass over." I had a walking-stick in my hand, and I was going along, and I just caught hold of his right hand, and he said, "Old man, don't you hold me that way; let me go, you damn son of a bitch, I will kill you;" and he struck me, and I went for the marshal to get him, but by this time four other men crowded on me. They were stout men, and they gathered on me and took me loose. I was on him, holding him down, and the first one came and tried to get my arm loose so I couldn't hold him, and then two others ran in and gathered on me, and finally the fourth one came up and shook me back against the wall, and one fellow jerked my hand loose from him, and Mr. Parker, the intendant of the town, and the marshal came there and hushed them, and got us separated; that was last Monday. He said, "I want to kill him, he is a damn democrat, and I want to kill him anyhow." Mr. Parker told him to go away; he says, "Less have no fuss at all." The doctor came and examined my head, and put a plaster on it.

Q. Have you any other fact you could state like this you have been stating to us?—A. No, sir; I can't give any other facts, only I have heard a great many threats, and I know that I am 'buked and discounted.

CROSS-EXAMINATION.

By Mr. CAMERON:

Q. You stated that the reason you left the republican party and joined the democratic party was because the members of the legislature and county officers in your county were incompetent?—A. Yes, sir; that first.

Q. What members of the legislature were incompetent, in your opinion; what are their names?—A. Ellison Cain.

Q. Where was he from?—A. From Abbeville.

Q. Of what legislature was he a member?—A. The legislature here.

Q. When?—A. Well, it has been four years back; he wa'n't in the last two years, but he sat here four sessions.

Q. He has not been a member for the last two years?—A. Not in the last two years, not for the last two years. I had been looking after it from 1868.

Q. Now, what other persons?—A. Cain, a colored man.

Q. When was he a member of the legislature?—A. Two years back.

Q. From what place?—A. From Abbeville.

By Mr. CHRISTIANCY:

Q. Is he a member now?—A. No, sir.

By Mr. CAMERON:

Q. Of how many legislatures was he a member?—A. He was in two, I think.

Q. When did he go out?—A. He went out the campaign before this last. He wa'n't elected in the campaign before the last; didn't get in.

Q. A year ago last fall he was not elected?—A. No, sir.

Q. Do you mean at the last election he was not elected, or a year ago?—A. Two years ago; he has been out two years.

Q. Who else?—A. Martin.

Q. Where is he from?—A. Abbeville.

Q. When was he a member of the legislature?—A. The same one Cain was in; he failed to get elected two years back.

Q. Who else?—A. Guffin.

Q. You say he was not fit to be a member of the legislature?—A. Yes, sir; I claimed that.

Q. When was he a member of the legislature?—A. Well, one of them was a member four years ago.

Q. One of the Guffins?—A. Yes, sir; then he was elected sheriff; two years ago the other Guffin was elected. I claimed that of all of them.

Q. That neither was fit for it?—A. Yes, sir; I claimed that neither of them was; that is they showed it at the time.

Q. Who else?—A. Wideman, from Abbeville.

Q. When was he a member of the legislature?—A. I think he was a member four sessions, and was a member the last two years. I think he was re-elected two years ago; I think he was a member two years before that, and I think he was re elected two years ago, and offered to run again in this last campaign.

Q. Who else?—A. Stullin—have been in, but he is not now; he was four years ago.

Q. From where?—A. From Abbeville.

Q. Who else?—A. I don't remember any others.

Q. Those are all?—A. Yes, sir; five of them—no, Holland—he is from Abbeville; there's two more, Coggins and Holland was in the last two years passed, and Coggins failed to get elected four years ago, and two years ago he were elected.

Q. When did you come to the conclusion that those men were not fit to be members of the legislature?—A. Well, sir, I have been getting more and more—

Q. When did you come to that conclusion, that these men were incompetent to discharge the duties of members of the legislature?—A. Well, a year ago, or a portion of it; well, I can go back two years and then—

Q. Wait one moment; whom did you come to the conclusion two years ago was incompetent?—A. I didn't consider any of them was, from the circumstances—

Q. That is, you came to the conclusion two years ago that all of them were unfit for that office?—A. Not all of them.

Q. What did you mean, then, when you said you came to the conclusion two years ago that all of them were unfit, and that you came to the conclusion since that time that others were not, but now you say that you came to the conclusion two years ago that none of them were fit for it?—A. Two years ago I didn't come to the conclusion that all of them was unfit, but two years ago I did that some of them were; and, in fact, I have been watching for four years.

Q. What I am trying to get at is, when did you come to the conclusion that these men were not fit to discharge the duties of representatives?—A. This spring last.

Q. That is the first time, is it?—A. No, sir; that is not the first time.

Q. When did you come to the conclusion first?—A. I have been looking at the thing, and studying about that for four years, have been picking the best material, and voting for them, and I have voted for one or two republicans.

Q. That is not answering my question; when did you first come to the conclusion that these men were not competent to discharge the duties of representatives?—A. I have been coming more and more to it for four years—have been picking the best till I come to the conclusion that there was none good.

Q. You came to that conclusion, that none of them were good?—A. Yes; none of them was fit.

Q. When did you come to that conclusion?—A. I came to that conclusion this last spring, that I never would vote for none of them no more. The thing grew worse and worse.

Q. Then you came to the conclusion last spring that none of these men were fit to be members of the legislature?—A. Yes, sir.

Q. And that is the reason you left the republican party?—A. I then said I would—

Q. I didn't ask you what you said; I ask you is that the reason you left the republican party?—A. Then I said that I wouldn't vote for them no more, that I would vote for somebody else.

Q. Now, I will ask you the question again: Did you leave the republican party because you came to the conclusion that these men were not competent to sit as members of the legislature?—A. I said I wouldn't vote for them—

Q. I will ask you the question again: Did you leave the republican party for that reason? Can you answer that question or not?—A. Yes, sir; and there's a great many other things besides that I have sawed.

Q. What offices have you held?—A. Nothing, sir, but a hammer in my hand and an anvil.

Q. Have you been a candidate for any office?—A. No, sir; never have been offered for a candidate for any office.

Q. For whom do you work mostly, white or colored men?—A. I work for all.

Q. For whom do you work mostly?—A. I work mostly for white men, because the shops that I occupy—

Q. I do not ask you for any reason, I just ask you for the fact.—A. Those are white men's shops. Now and then some black men would come in and fetch me some work, and some white men would have me hired by the day, and I would take up some of the blacksmith-work at night and do that extra, and make some extra.

Q. For whom do you work mostly, white or black men?—A. I work mostly for white men.

Q. Who pays you the most money for your work?—A. White men. I think, sir, I can show you $200 now that I have against black men that have not paid. I kept a public shop two years ago in the town of Abbeville, fifty yards from my house, and I believe that there's thirty-odd dollars owing me by white men, and $224 owing by black men.

By Mr. CHRISTIANCY:

Q. The whites pay and the black men do not?—A. Yes, sir; the reason the white man ain't paid this $30, he is dead, and the estate has not been settled, and there is $224 or $222 against the colored people now.

Q. Why do you not collect the money that the colored men owe you?

The WITNESS. Why don't I collect?

Mr. CHRISTIANCY. Yes.—A. Well, it seems like you can answer that question. I might say why don't you get blood out of a turnip. I can't collect it; it ain't in them, and I can't get it.

Q. Have they any property out of which you could collect it?—A. I entreated them, and I have toted my books after them until I am ashamed. I have toted my accounts drawn off from my books until the account would get all dirty and worn-out, carrying it around and showing, and I would have to go to some gentleman to get it renewed; and they have come to the conclusion that they won't pay me at all; that I am a democrat, and they say, "We never allowed to pay it," and I can't get it out of them.

Q. You do not collect it because you cannot get it out of them?—A. Well, I can't get it; them that could pay me something won't do it.

By Mr. CAMERON:

Q. You said that some one told you that he would knock you to hell in a minute?—A. Yes, sir.

Q. Are you a member of the church?—A. Yes, sir.

Q. Do you think he could knock you to hell?—A. No, sir; I don't think he could do it. I know he couldn't knock me to hell, but I knowed he could knock me somewhere else; that it might feel like the Universalist hell.

Q. Did you hear any democrats say to colored republicans, when they were trying to get them to vote the democratic ticket, that if they voted the radical ticket they would discharge them from their employ, and that they would turn them off their lands?—A. No, sir.

Q. Heard nothing of that kind?—A. No, sir; nothing of that sort at all.

By Mr. CHRISTIANCY:

Q. You never made use of any such argument to the colored people?—A. No, sir; I am satisfied, because I have to employ myself.

Tom Lomax—Abbeville County.

[Ten years old when the Civil War began, this black farmer switched to the Democratic Party, where he was recognized for his leadership abilities.]

COLUMBIA, S.C., *January* 3, 1877.

TOM LOMAX (colored) sworn and examined.

By Mr. MERRIMON:

Question. What is your age?—Answer. I am going on twenty-six years old.

Q. Where do you live?—A. I live in Lowndesville.

Q. What is your business?—A. Farming.

Q. What political party do you belong to?—A. I belong to the democratic party.

Q. Where were you on the day of the last election?—A. I was at Lowndesville.

Q. What ticket did you vote on that day?—A. I voted the democratic ticket.

Q. Did anybody force you to do it?—A. No, sir.

Q. Did you belong to the democratic club there?—A. Yes, sir.

Q. Were you forced to join that?—A. No, sir.

Q. Did you join it of your own free will?—A. Yes, sir; of my own free will.

Q. State whether you saw any armed men at the poll that day?—A. yes, sir; I saw two colored men come up to one of the polls; they had double-barreled shot-guns, and Burt Griffin, he had a pistol; the United States marshal, I believe, they called him.

Q. Did you see any white men have arms?—A. If they did have them they had them very close; I didn't see them.

Q. Have you ever been insulted or abused or ridiculed by colored republicans for being a democrat?—A. Yes, sir.

Q. State what was done to you.—A. I was riding out one day, and they said, "O, you colored democrats; by the time we have done with you all they will have you in slavery. You are a pack of damned fools," and the women there, they said, "You can kiss my arse," and they flung their coats over their heads and commenced kicking up their legs and sticking them out at us, and I walked out without paying any attention.

Q. What did the colored women do, if anything?—A. They turned up their coats and told us to kiss their arse.

Q. Well, when was that?—A. I don't know exactly what time it was now. I never kept no particular account of it. It was a while before the election. It was about the same time that they had a big time speaking up at Lowndesville. It was about, I suppose, three weeks, or may be a month, or two months, I expect, before the election.

Q. Now, which was it, three weeks, a month, or two months?—A. I really couldn't state now about what time it was.

Q. How large a republican meeting was there?—A. Well, there was about between fifty and seventy-five men there, I reckon.

Q. Who were the speakers at that meeting?—A. Henry Heard was there for one, and Tom Heard, and they was looking for some white men from Abbeville. They said Mr. Tolbert would be there, Tom Tolbert.

Q. Well, who were there as speakers?—A. After them white folks came there, and told them to go to Lowndesville, they said, "We ain't going to have no meeting," being as the white folks were there, and they said, "We will put it off, and go home." The white folks said, "No, go on with your meeting, and we will stay here, if you won't go to ours," and we said, "No, we ain't going to have it to-day."

Q. So the colored people didn't have any speaking at that time?—A. No, sir.

Q. Were you there acting as a republican then?—A. O, yes, sir.

Q. When did you attend the republican meeting?—A. They held one over there at Hal Belcher's.

Q. How long was that after this meeting that you have spoken of?—A. Well, it was about a week and three or four days; somewhere along there.

Q. How large a meeting was that?—A. There was about twenty-five or thirty men there.

Q. Were you there?—A. Yes, sir.

Q. Were you republican then?—A. Yes, sir; I made a speech there that day myself.

Q. When did you attend the next republican meeting?—A. Well, we never held nary another one up in Lowndesville to my knowins—back in the country where I live—I live sort of away back on the other side of Lowndesville.

Q. Did you attend any more political meetings?—A. No, sir; I didn't attend no more.

Q. Have you ever been a candidate for any office?—A. No, sir.

Q. You never wanted any office, did you?—A. O, yes, sir; I would have liked to have got hold of one if I could.

Q. But the colored people would not give you any?—A. No; I never tried for nary one, because I didn't think I was capable of filling an office.

CROSS-EXAMINATION.

By Mr. CHRISTIANCY:

Q. At that time, then, did you leave the republican party?—A. Well, I left the republican party up about—somewhere about a month before the election.

Q. Whose plantation was that you lived on?—A. James Lomax.

Q. You say he didn't live on it himself?—A. No, sir.

Q. And that all the people who lived on it were colored people?—A. Yes, sir.

Q. Did they also vote the democratic ticket?—A. No, sir.

Q. None of them?—A. None of them voted the straight-out democrat ticket. Some of them voted for Mr. Hampton, and that was all. There was three or four of them, I think, voted for Mr. Hampton.

Q. How many of them are there altogether on that plantation of colored people?—A. There is about—I could not tell how many there is.

Q. Colored voters, I mean.—A. Colored voters, about twenty, I reckon.

Q. How many of them voted for Hampton?—A. There was three of them voted for Mr. Hampton.

Q. Well, sir, they are all alive there yet, I suppose?—A. yes, sir.

Q. Who was it persuaded you to go into the democratic party?—A. No one at all.

Q. Nobody?—A. No one did not.

Q. Well, sir, do you know that a good many of these colored people went into the democratic party because they could get their land better and get their employment more certainly if they went than if they went with the republicans?—A. No, sir; I never heard that mentioned at all.

Q. Who owns the land there? Are there no republican land-owners there?—A. Yes, sir; there is a man at Abbeville, Mr. John R. Tolbert, who owns a large plantation.

Q. What is he?—A. He is a republican.

Q. Most of the land-owners there are democrats, are they not?—A. Yes, sir.

Q. Most of the men of property are democrats, are they not?—A. O, yes, sir.

Q. The colored people look more to the democrats for employment than they do to the republicans?—A. Well, of course, they are living right there with the democrats. There ain't no republicans there got no land. They have got none there, as far as we is concerned.

Q. How do the democrats treat you?—A. They have always treated me splendidly.

Q. Especially since you joined them?—A. They treat me just like they always did—treat me well.

Q. Who did you see before you came here?—A. After I came here?

Q. Yes, who inquired of you what you were going to testify to?—A. Nobody, only when I came up-stairs there was a black man standing by the door, who asked me what did I want here, and I said I was sent for to come here, and he asked me for which side did I come, and I told him that they sent for me to come for something about the election, I didn't know exactly what. He says, "I know; you are a democrat." I says, "Why?" He says, "I know from the way you talk you are a democrat, and you just came here to swear against your own color." I said, "No, I didn't come here to swear against my own color; I came here to swear the truth. Do you believe if am put on my oath I would swear a lie?"

Q. Did he tell you what you could swear to?—A. This 'ere colored man down here, he axed me—

Q. You did not tell anybody else?—A. No, sir; nobody axed me anything else about it.

Q. Nobody took down any memorandum of your testimony before you came here?—A. None but this colored man out there.

Q. Have you not seen General Butler since you came here?—A. Yes, sir.

Q. Did he not ask you what you could swear to?—A. O, of course, when I went up-stairs.

Q. That is what I was talking about exactly.—A. I did not understand.

Q. Did he not take down a memorandum of what you could swear to?—A. He axed me what was my testimony, and I just—he didn't ax me no questions, only he axed me my testimony. He wanted to see what I knew about it, and I told him what I knowed about it myself.

Q. Is he the only one that you told what you could testify to?—A. Yes, sir; O, yes, sir, he was the onus one.

SOUTH CAROLINA SLAVE NARRATIVES

Project #1655
W. W. Dixon
Winnsboro, S.C.

Frank Adamson
Ex-Slave 82 Years Old.

[A child of six at the outbreak of the Civil War, Adamson belonged to a powerful Fairfield County family. Explaining his actions during Reconstruction, he described himself as "black as a crow" but with "a white folks heart."]

"I 'members when you was barefoot at de bottom; now I see you a settin' dere, gittin' bare at de top, as bare as de palm of my hand.

"I's been 'possum huntin' wid your pappy, when he lived on de Wateree, just after de war. One night us got into tribulation, I tells you! 'Twas 'bout midnight when de dogs make a tree. Your pappy climb up de tree, git 'bout halfway up, heard sumpin' dat once you hears it you never forgits, and dats de rattlin' of de rattles on a rattle snake's tail. Us both 'stinctly hear dat sound! What us do? Me on de ground, him up de tree, but where de snake? Dat was de misery, us didn't know. Dat snake give us fair warnin' though! Marster Sam (dats your pa) 'low: 'Frank, ease down on de ground; I'll just stay up here for a while.' I lay on them leaves, skeered to make a russle. Your pa up de tree skeered to go up or down! Broad daylight didn't move us. Sun come up, he look all 'round from his vantage up de tree, then come down, not 'til then, do I gits on my foots.

"Then I laugh and laugh and laugh, and ask Marster Sam how he felt. Marster Sam kinda frown and say: 'Damn I feels like hell! Git up dat tree! Don't you see dat 'possum up dere?' I say: 'But where de snake, Marster?' He say: 'Dat rattler done gone home, where me and you and dat 'possum gonna be pretty soon!'

"I b'longs to de Peays. De father of them all was, Kershaw Peay. My marster was his son, Nicholas; he was a fine man to just look at. My mistress was always tellin' him 'bout how fine and handsome-like he was. He must of got use to it; howsomever, marster grin every time she talk like dat.

"My pappy was bought from de Adamson peoples; they say they got him off de ship from Africa. He sho' was a man; he run all de other niggers 'way from my mammy and took up wid her widout askin' de marster. Her name was Lavinia. When us got free, he 'sisted on Adamson was de name us would go by. He name was William Adamson. Yes sir! my brothers was: Justus, Hillyard, and Donald, and my sisters was, Martha and Lizzettie.

"Deed I did work befo' freedom. What I do? Hoed cotton, pick cotton, 'tend to calves and slop de pigs, under de 'vision of de overseer. Who he was? First one name Mr. Cary, he a good man. Another one Mr. Tim Gladden, burn you up whenever he just take a notion to pop his whip. Us boys run 'round in our shirt tails. He lak to see if he could lift de shirt tail widout techin' de skin. Just as often as not, though, he tech de skin. Little boy holler and Marster Tim laugh.

"Us live in quarters. Our beds was nailed to de sides of de house. Most of de chillun slept on pallets on de floor. Got water from a big spring.

"De white folks 'tend to you all right. Us had two doctors, Doctor Carlisle and Doctor James.

"I see some money, but never own any then. Had plenty to eat: Meat, bread, milk, lye hominy, horse apples, turnips, collards, pumpkins, and dat kind of truck.

"Was marster rich? How come he wasn't? He brag his land was ten miles square and he had a thousand slaves. Them poor white folks looked up to him lak God Almighty; they sho' did. They would have stuck their hands in de fire if he had of asked them to do it. He had a fish pond on top of de house and terraces wid strawberries, all over de place. See them big rock columns down dere now? Dats all dats left of his grandness and greatness. They done move de whippin' post dat was in de backyard. Yes sah, it was a 'cessity wid them niggers. It stood up and out to 'mind them dat if they didn't please de master and de overseer, they'd hug dat post, and de lend of dat whip lash gwine to flip to de hide of dat back of their's.

"I ain't a complainin'. He was a good master, bestest in de land, but he just have to have a whippin' post, 'cause you'll find a whole passle of bad niggers when you gits a thousand of them in one flock.

"Screech owl holler? Women and men turn socks and stockings wrong side out quick, dat they did, do it now, myself. I's black as a crow but I's got a white folks heart. Didn't ketch me foolin' 'round wid niggers in radical times. I's as close to white folks then as peas in a pod. Wore de red shirt and drunk a heap of brandy in Columbia, dat time us went down to [put] General Hampton into power. I 'clare I hollered so loud goin' 'long in de procession, dat a nice white lady run out one of de houses down dere in Columbia, give me two biscuits and a drum stick of chicken, patted me on de shoulder, and say: 'Thank God for all de big black men dat can holler for Governor Hampton as loud as dis one does.' Then I hollers some more for to please dat lady, though I had to take de half chawed chicken out dis old mouth, and she laugh 'bout dat 'til she cried. She did!

"Well, I'll be rockin' 'long balance of dese days, a hollerin' for Mr. Roosevelt, just as loud as I holler then for Hampton.

"My young marsters was: Austin, Tom, and Nicholas; they was all right 'cept they tease you too hard maybe some time, and want to mix in wid de 'fairs of slave 'musements.

"Now what make you ask dat? Did me ever do any courtin'? You knows I did. Every he thing from a he king down to a bunty rooster gits 'cited 'bout she things. I's lay wake many nights 'bout sich things. It's de nature of a he, to take after de she. They do say dat a he angel ain't got dis to worry 'bout.

"I fust courted Martha Harrison. Us marry and jine de church. Us had nine chillun; seven of them livin'. A woman can't stand havin' chillun, lak a man. Carryin', sucklin', and 'tending to them wore her down, dat, wid de malaria of de Wateree brung her to her grave.

"I sorrow over her for weeks, maybe five months, then I got to thinking how I'd pair up wid dis one and dat one and de other one. Took to shavin' again and gwine to Winnsboro every Saturday, and different churches every Sunday. I hear a voice from de choir, one Sunday, dat makes me sit up and take notice of de gal on de off side in front. Well sir! a spasm of fright fust hit me dat I might not git her, dat I was too old for de likes of her, and dat some no 'count nigger might be in de way. In a few minutes I come to myself. I rise right up, walked into dat choir, stand by her side, and wid dis voice of mine, dat always 'tracts 'tention, jined in de hymn and out sung them all. It was easy from dat time on.

"I marry Kate at de close of dat revival. De day after de weddin', what you reckon? Don't know? Well, after gittin' breakfas' she went to de field, poke 'round her neck, basket on her head and picked two hundred pounds of cotton. Dats de kind of woman she is."

Project #1655
W. W. Dixon
Winnsboro, S.C.

Charley Barber
Ex-Slave 81 Years Old.

[Only five years old when the Civil War began, Barber could still recall the "special vengeance" the Yankees had for his white folks in Chester County. In 1876 he left the plantation for Winnsboro in Fairfield County to become a railroad hand. Landing this job, buying a red shirt, and voting for Hampton were the first "big thing(s)" he did in his life.]

Charley Barber lives in a shanty kind of house, situated on a plot of ground containing two acres all his own. It is a mile and a half southeast of Winnsboro, S.C. He lives with an anaemic daughter, Maggie, whose chief interests are a number of cats, about the premises, and a brindled, crumple-horned cow that she ties out to graze every morning and milks at evening.

Charley is squat of figure, short neck, popeyed, and has white hair. He tills the two acres and produces garden truck that he finds a sale for among the employees of the Winnsboro mills, just across the railroad from his home. He likes to talk, and pricks up his ears, (so to speak), whenever anything is related as having occurred in the past. He will importune those present to hear his version of the event unusual.

"Well sah, dis is a pleasure to have you call 'pon me, howsomever it be unexpected dis mornin'. Shoo! (driving the chickens out of the house) Shoo! Cit out of here and go scratch a livin' for them chickens dat's followin' you yet, and you won't wean and git to layin' again. Fust thing you know you'll be spoilin' de floor, when us is got company dis very minute. Seat! Maggie, git them cats out de chairs long 'nough for Mr. Wood [Woodward] to set in one whilst he's come to see me dis mornin'.

"And dat's it? You wants me to talk over de days dat am gone? How dis come 'bout and how dat come 'bout, from de day I was born, to dis very hour? Let's light up our smokestacks befo' us begin. Maybe you wants a drink of water. Maggie, fetch de water here!

"How old you think I is, sixty-five? My goodness! Do you hear dat Maggie? (Rubbing his hands; his eyes shining with pleasure) Take another look and make another guess. Seventy-five? You is growin' warm but you'll have to come again!

"Bless your soul Marse Wood, you know what old Mudder Shifton say? She 'low dat: 'In de year 1881, de world to an end will surely come'. I was twenty-five years old, when all de niggers and most of de white folks was believin' dat old lady and lookin' for de world to come to an end in 1881. Dat was de year dat I jined de church, 'cause I wanted to make sure dat if de end did come, I'd be caught up in dat rapture dat de white Methodist preacher was preachin' 'bout and explainin' to my marster and mistress at deir house on de piazza dat year.

"I is eighty-one years old. I was born up on de Wateree River, close to

Great Falls. My marster was Ozmond Barber. My mistress was name Miss Elizabeth; her de wife of Marse Ozmond. My pappy was name Jacob. My mammy went by de name of Jemima. They both come from Africa where they was born. They was 'ticed on a ship, fetch 'cross de ocean to Virginny, fetch to Winnsboro by a slave drover, and sold to my marster's father. Dat what they tell me. When they was sailin' over, dere was five or six hundred others all together down under de first deck of de ship, where they was locked in. They never did talk lak de other slaves, could just say a few words, use deir hands, and make signs. They want deir collards, turnips, and deir 'tators, raw. They lak sweet milk so much they steal it.

"Pappy care nothin' 'bout clothes and wouldn't wear shoes in de winter time or any time. It was 'ginst de law to bring them over here when they did, I learn since. But what is de law now and what was de law then, when bright shiny money was in sight? Money make de automobile go. Money make de train go. Money make de mare go, and at dat time I 'spect money make de ships go. Yes sir, they, my pappy and mammy, was just smuggled in dis part of de world, I bet you!

"War come on, my marster went out as a captain of de Horse Marines. A tune was much sung by de white folks on de place and took wid de niggers. It went lak dis:

'I'm Captain Jenks of de Horse Marines
I feed my horse on corn and beans.
Oh! I'm Captain Jenks of de Horse Marines
And captain in de army!'

"When de Yankees come they seem to have special vengeance for my white folks. They took everything they could carry off and burnt everything they couldn't carry off.

"Mistress and de chillun have to go to Chester to git a place to sleep and eat, wid kinfolks. De niggers just lay 'round de place 'til master rode in, after de war, on a horse; him have money and friends and git things goin' agin. I stay on dere 'til '76. Then I come to Winnsboro and git a job as section hand laborer on de railroad. Out of de fust money,—(I git paid off de pay train then; company run a special pay train out of Columbia to Charlotte. They stop at every station and pay de hands off at de rear end of de train in cash). Well, as I was a sayin': Out de fust money, I buys me a red shirt and dat November I votes and de fust vote I put in de box was for Governor Wade Hampton. Dat was de fust big thing I done.

"De nex' big thing I done was fall in love wid Mary Wylie. Dat come 'bout on de second pay day. De other nigger gals say her marry me for my money but I never have believed it. White ladies do dat 'kalkilating' trick sometime but you take a blue-gum nigger gal, all wool on de top of her head and lak to dance and jig wid her foots, to pattin' and fiddle music, her ain't gonna have money in de back of her head when her pick out a man to marry. Her gonna want a man wid muscles on his arms and back and I had them. Usin' dat pick and shovel on de railroad just give me what it took to git Mary. Us had ten chillun. Some dead, some marry and leave. My wife die year befo' last. Maggie is puny, as you see, and us gits 'long wid de goodness of de Lord and de white folks.

"I b'longs to de St. John Methodist Church in Middlesix, part of Winnsboro. They was havin' a rival (revival) meetin' de night of de earthquake, last day of August, in 1886. Folks had hardly got over de scare of 1881, 'bout de world comin' to an end. It was on Tuesday night, if I don't disremember, 'bout 9 o'clock. De preacher was prayin', just after de fust sermon, but him never got to de amen part of dat prayer. Dere come a noise or rumblin', lak far off thunder, seem lak it come from de northwest, then de church begin to rock lak a baby's cradle. Dere was great excitement. Old Aunt Melvina holler: 'De world comin' to de end'. De preacher say: 'Oh, Lordy', and run out of de pulpit. Everybody run out de church in de moonlight. When de second quake come, 'bout a minute after de fust, somebody started up de cry: 'De devil under de church! De devil under de church! De devil gwine to take de church on his back and run away wid de church!' People never stop runnin' 'til they got to de court house in town. Dere they, 'clare de devil done take St. John's Church on his back and fly away to hell wid it. Marse Henry Galliard make a speech and tell them what it was and beg them to go home. Dat Mr. Skinner, de telegraph man at de depot, say de main part of it was way down 'bout Charleston, too far away for anybody to git hurt here, 'less a brick from a chimney fall on somebody's head. De niggers mostly believes what a fine man, lak Marse Henry, tell them. De crowd git quiet. Some of them go home but many of them, down in de low part of town, set on de railroad track in de moonlight, all night. I was mighty sleepy de nex' mornin' but

I work on de railroad track just de same. Dat night folks come back to St. John's Church, find it still dere, and such a outpourin' of de spirit was had as never was had befo' or since.

"Just think! Dat has been fifty-one years ago. Them was de glorious horse and buggy days. Dere was no air-ships, no autos and no radios. White folks had horses to drive. Niggers had mules to ride to a baseball game, to see white folks run lak de patarollers (patrollers) was after them and they holler lak de world was on fire."

Project #1655
W. W. Dixon
Winnsboro, S.C.

Ed Barber
Ex-Slave 77 Years Old.

[Born in 1860 near Winnsboro in Fairfield County, this farmer, who described himself as half white and half black, sided with the Democrats because he knew "which side de butter was on de bread."]

Ed Barber lives in a small one-room house in the midst of a cotton field on the plantation of Mr. A. M. Owens, ten miles southeast of Winnsboro, S.C. He lives alone and does his own cooking and housekeeping. He is a bright mulatto, has an erect carriage and posture, appears younger than his age, is intelligent and enjoys recounting the tales of his lifetime. His own race doesn't give him much countenance. His friends in the old days of reconstruction were white people. He presumes on such past affiliation and considers himself better than the full-blooded Negro.

"It's been a long time since I see you. Maybe you has forgot but I ain't forgot de fust time I put dese lookers on you, in '76. Does you 'members dat day? It was in a piece of pines beyond de Presbyterian Church, in Winnsboro, S.C. Us both had red shirts. You was a ridin' a gray pony and I was aridin' a red mule, sorrel like. You say dat wasn't '76? Well, how come it wasn't? Ouillah Harrison, another nigger, was dere, though he was a man. Both of us got to arguin'. He 'low he could vote for Hampton and I couldn't, 'cause I wasn't 21. You say it was '78 'stead of '76, dat day in de pines when you was dere? Well! Well! I sho' been thinkin' all dis time it was '76.

"'Member de fight dat day when Mr. Pole Barnadore knock Mr. Blanchard down, while de speakin' was a gwine on? You does? Well, us come to common 'greement on dat, bless God!

"Them was a scary times! Me bein' just half nigger and half white man, I knowed which side de butter was on de bread. Who I see dere? Well, dere was a string of red shirts a mile long, dat come into Winnsboro from White Oak. And another from Flint Hill, over de Pea Ferry road, a mile long. De barrooms of de town did a big business dat day. Seem lak it was de fashion to git drunk all 'long them days.

"Them red shirts was de monkey wrench in de cotton-gin of de carpet bag party. I's here to tell you. If a nigger git hungry, all he have to do is go to de white folk's house, beg for a red shirt, and explain hisself a democrat. He might not git de shirt right then but he git his belly full of everything de white folks got, and de privilege of comin' to dat trough sometime agin.

"You wants me to tell you 'bout who I is, where I born, and how old I is? Well, just cross examine me and I'll tell you de facts as best I knows how.

"I was born twelve miles east of Winnsboro, S.C. My marster say it was de 18th of January, 1860.

"My mother name Ann. Her b'long to my marster, James Barber. Dat's not a fair question when you ask me who my daddy was. Well, just say he was a white man and dat my mother never did marry nobody, while he lived. I was de onliest child my mother ever had.

"After freedom my mother raised me on de Marse Adam Barber place, up by Rocky Mount and Mitford. I stayed dere 'til all de 'citement of politics die down. My help was not wanted so much at de 'lection boxes, so I got to roamin' 'round to fust one place and then another. But wheresomever I go, I kept a thinkin' 'bout Rosa and de ripe may-pops in de field in cotton pickin' time. I landed back to de Barber place and after a skirmish or two wid de old folks, marry de gal de Lord always 'tended for me to marry. Her name was Rosa Ford. You ask me if she was pretty? Dat's a strange thing. Do you ever hear a white person say a colored woman is pretty? I never have but befo' God when I was trampin' 'round Charleston, dere was a church dere called St. Mark, dat all de society folks of my color went to. No black nigger welcome dere, they told me. Thinkin' as how I was bright 'nough to git in, I up and goes dere one Sunday. Ah, how they did carry on, bow and scrape and ape de white folks. I see some pretty feathers, pretty fans, and pretty women dere! I was uncomfortable all de time though, 'cause they was too 'hifalootin' in de ways, in de singin', and all sorts of carryin' ons.

"Glad you fetch me back to Rosa. Us marry and had ten chillun. Francis, Thompkins, William, Jim, Levi, Ab and Oz is dead. Katie marry a Boykin and is livin' in New York. My wife, Rosa, die on dis place of Mr. Owens.

"I lives in a house by myself. I hoes a little cotton, picks plums and blackberries but dewberries 'bout played out.

"My marster, James Barber, went through de Civil War and died. I begs you, in de name of de good white folks of '76 and Wade Hampton, not to forget me in dis old age pension business.

"What I think of Abe Lincoln? I think he was a poor buckra white man, to de likes of me. Although, I 'spects Mr. Lincoln meant well but I can't help but wish him had continued splittin' them fence rails, which they say he knowed all 'bout, and never took a hand in runnin' de government of which he knowed nothin' 'bout. Marse Jeff Davis was all right, but him oughta got out and fought some, lak General Lee, General Jackson and 'Poleon Bonaparte. Us might have won de war if he had turned up at some of de big battles lak Gettysburg, 'Chickenmaroger', and 'Applemattox'. What you think 'bout dat?

"Yes sah, I has knowed a whole lot of good white men. Marse General Bratton, Marse Ed P. Mobley, Marse Will Durham, dat owned dis house us now settin' in, and Dr. Henry Gibson. Does I know any good colored men? I sho' does! Dere's Professor Benjamin Russell at Blackstock. You knows him. Then dere was Ouillah Harrison, dat own a four-hoss team and a saddle hoss, in red shirt days. One time de brass band at Winnsboro, S.C. wanted to go to Camden, S.C. to play at de speakin' of Hampton. He took de whole band from Winnsboro to Camden, dat day, free of charge. Ah! De way dat band did play all de way to Ridgeway, down de road to Longtown, cross de Camden Ferry, and right into de town. Dere was horns a blowin', drums a beatin', and people a shoutin': 'Hurrah for Hampton!' Some was a singin': 'Hang Dan Chamberlain on a Sour Apple Tree'. Ouillah come home and found his wife had done had a boy baby. What you reckon? He name dat boy baby, Wade Hampton. When he come home to die, he lay his hand on dat boy's head and say: 'Wade, 'member who you name for and always vote a straight out democrat ticket'. Which dat boy did!"

Project #1655
W. W. Dixon
Winnsboro, S.C.

Andy Brice
Ex-Slave 81 Years Old.

[Born just five years before the Civil War, Brice hated the way the Yankees had treated white and black women. Every Yankee he saw had the "stamp of poor white trash." In 1876 when he wore the red shirt, black Republicans called him "a white folks nigger."]

Andy Brice lives with his wife and two small children, about twelve miles east of Ridgeway, S.C., in a two-room frame building, chimney in the center. The house is set in a little cluster of pines one hundred and fifty yards north of state highway #34. Andy, since the amputation of his right leg five years ago, has done no work and is too old to learn a trade. He has a regular beggar's route including the towns of Ridgeway, Winnsboro, Woodward, and Blackstock. His amiability and good nature enable him to go home after each trip with a little money and pack of miscellaneous gifts from white friends.

"Howdy Cap'n! I come to Winnsboro dis mornin' from way 'cross Wateree, where I live now 'mongst de bull-frogs and skeeters. Seem lak they just sing de whole night thru: 'De bull-frog on de bank, and de skeeter in de pool.' Then de skeeter sail 'round my face wid de tra la, la la la, la la la part of dat old song you is heard, maybe many times.

"I see a spit-box over dere. By chance, have you got any 'bacco? Make me more glib if I can chew and spit; then I 'members more and better de things done past and gone.

"I was a slave of Mistress Jane. Her was a daughter of old Marster William Brice. Her marry Henry Younge and mammy was give to Marse Henry and Miss Jane.

"My pappy name Tony. Mammy name Sallie. You is seen her a many a day. Marse Henry got kilt in de war. His tombstone and Mistress Jane's tombstone am in Concord Cemetery. They left two chillun, Miss Kittie and Miss Maggie. They both marry a Caldwell; same name but no kin. Miss Kittie marry Marse Joe Caldwell and move to Texas. Miss Maggie marry Marse Camel Caldwell and move to North Carolina.

"My pappy die durin' de war. After freedom, mammy marry a ugly, no 'count nigger name Mills Douglas. She had one child by him, name Janie. My mammy name her dat out of memory and love for old mistress, in slavery time. I run away from de home of my step-pappy and got work wid Major Thomas Brice. I work for him 'til I become a full grown man and come to be de driver of de four-hoss wagon.

"One day I see Marse Thomas a twistin' de ears on a fiddle and rosinin' de bow. Then he pull dat bow 'cross de belly of dat fiddle. Sumpin' bust loose in me and sing all thru my head and tingle in my fingers. I make up my mind, right then and dere, to save and buy me a fiddle. I got one dat Christmas, bless God! I learn and been playin' de fiddle ever since. I pat one foot while I playin'. I kept on playin' and pattin' dat foot for thirty years. I lose dat foot in a smash up wid a highway accident but I play de old tunes on dat fiddle at night, dat foot seem to be dere at de end of dat leg (indicating) and pats just de same. Sometime I ketch myself lookin' down to see if it have come back and jined itself up to dat leg, from de very charm of de music I makin' wid de fiddle and de bow.

"I never was very popular wid my own color. They say behind my back, in '76, dat I's a white folks nigger. I wear a red shirt then, drink red liquor, play de fiddle at de 'lection box, and vote de white folks ticket. Who I marry? I marry Ellen Watson, as pretty a ginger cake nigger as ever fried a batter cake or rolled her arms up in a wash tub. How I git her? I never git her; dat fiddle got her. I play for all de white folks dances down at Cedar Shades, up at Blackstock. De money roll in when someone pass 'round de hat and say: 'De fiddler?' Ellen had more beaux 'round her than her could shake a stick at but de beau she lak best was de bow dat could draw music out of them five strings, and draw money into dat hat, dat jingle in my pocket de nex' day when I go to see her.

"I 'members very little 'bout de war, tho' I was a good size boy when de Yankees come. By instinct, a nigger can make up his mind pretty quick 'bout de creed of white folks, whether they am buckra or whether they am not. Every Yankee I see had de stamp of poor white trash on them. They strutted 'round, big Ike fashion, a bustin' in rooms widout knockin', talkin' free to de white ladies, and familiar to de slave gals, ransackin' drawers, and runnin' deir bayonets into feather beds, and into de flower beds in de yards.

"What church I b'long to? None. Dat fiddle draws down from hebben all de sermons dat I understan'. I sings de hymns in de way I praise and glorify de Lord.

"Cotton pickin' was de biggest work I ever did, outside of drivin' a wagon and playin' de fiddle. Look at them fingers; they is supple. I carry two rows of cotton at a time. One week I pick, in a race wid others, over 300 pounds a day. Commencin' Monday, thru Friday night, I pick 1,562 pounds cotton seed. Dat make a bale weighin' 500 pounds, in de lint.

"Ellen and me have one child, Sallie Ann. Ellen 'joy herself; have a good time nussin' white folks chillun. Nussed you; she tell me 'bout it many time. 'Spect she mind you of it very often. I knows you couldn't git 'round dat woman; nobody could. De Lord took her home fifteen years ago and I marry a widow, Ida Delton, down on de Kershaw County side.

"You wants me to tell 'bout dat 'lection day at Woodward, in 1878? You wants to know de beginnin' and de end of it? Yes? Well, you couldn't wet dis old man's whistle wid a swallow of red liquor now? Couldn't you or could you? Dis was de way of it: It was set for Tuesday. Monday I drive de four-hoss wagon down to dis very town. Marse John McCrory and Marse Ed Woodward come wid me. They was in a buggy. When us got here, us got twenty, sixteen shooters and put them under de hay us have in de wagon. Bar rooms was here. I had fetched my fiddle 'long and played in Marse Fred Habernick's bar 'til dinner time. Us leave town 'bout four o'clock. Roads was bad but us got home 'bout dark. Us put de guns in Marse Andy Mobley's store. Marse Ed and me leave Marse John to sleep in de store and to take care of de guns.

"De nex' mornin', polls open in de little school house by de brick church. I was dere on time, help to fix de table by de window and set de ballot boxes on it. Voters could come to de window, put deir arms thru and tuck de vote in a slit in de boxes. Dere was two supervisors, Marse Thomas for de democrats and Uncle Jordan for de radicals. Marse Thomas had a book and a pencil, Uncle Jordan had de same.

"Joe Foster, big buckra nigger, want to vote a stranger. Marse Thomas challenge dis vote. In them times colored preachers so 'furiate de women, dat they would put on breeches and vote de 'Publican radical ticket. De stranger look lak a woman. Joe Foster 'spute Marse Thomas' word and Marse Thomas knock him down wid de naked fist. Marse Irish Billy Brice, when him see four or five hindred blacks crowdin' 'round Marse Thomas, he jump thru de window from de inside. When he lit on de ground, pistol went off pow! One nigger drop in his tracks. Sixteen men come from nowhere and sixteen, sixteen shooters. Marse Thomas hold up his hand to them and say: 'Wait!' Him point to de niggers and say: 'Git.' They start to runnin' 'cross de railroad, over de hillside and never quit runnin' 'til they git half a mile away. De only niggers left on dat ground was me, old Uncle Kantz, (you know de old mulatto, club-foot nigger) well, me and him and Albert Gladney, de hurt nigger dat was shot thru de neck was de only niggers left. Dr. Tom Douglas took de ball out Albert's neck and de white folks put him in a wagon and sent him home. I drive de wagon. When I got back, de white boys was in de graveyard gittin' names off de tombstones to fill out de talley sheets, dere was so many votes in de box for de Hampton ticket, they had to vote de dead. I 'spect dat was one resurrection day all over South Carolina."

Project #1655
W. W. Dixon
Winnsboro, S.C.

John C. Brown and Adeline Brown Ex-Slaves 85 Years and 96 Years Old.

[Born to a white woman in 1852, Brown was not acknowledged by his black father until after the Civil War. Abused by his black stepmother, the teenager ran away to Robert Clowney's plantation in Fairfield County, where he was well treated. He supported his employer when Clowney entered politics.]

John C. Brown and his wife, Adeline, who is eleven years older than himself, live in a ramshackle four-room frame house in the midst of a cotton field, six miles west of Woodward, S.C. John assisted in laying the foundation and building the house forty-four years ago. A single china-berry tree, gnarled but stately, adds to, rather than detracts from, the loneliness of the dilapidated house. The premises and thereabout are owned by the Federal Land Bank. The occupants pay no rent. Neither of them are able to work. They have been fed by charity and the W.P.A. for the past eighteen months.

(John talking)

"Where and when I born? Well, dat'll take some 'hear say', Mister. I never knowed my mammy. They say she was a white lady dat visited my old marster and mistress. Dat I was found in a basket, dressed in nice baby clothes, on de railroad track at Dawkins, S.C. De engineer stop de train, got out, and found me sumpin' like de princess found Moses, but not in de bulrushes. Him turn me over to de conductor. De conductor carry me to de station at Dawkins, where Marse Tom Dawkins come to meet de train dat mornin' and claim me as found on his land. Him say him had de best right to me. De conductor didn't 'ject to dat. Marse Tom carry me home and give me to Miss Betsy. Dat was his wife and my mistress. Her always say dat Sheton Brown was my father. He was one of de slaves on de place; de carriage driver. After freedom he tell me he was my real pappy. Him took de name of Brown and dat's what I go by.

"My father was a ginger-bread colored man, not a full-blooded nigger. Dat's how I is altogether yallow. See dat lady over dere in dat chair? Dat's my wife. Her brighter skinned than I is. How come dat? Her daddy was a full-blooded Irishman. He come over here from Ireland and was overseer for Marse Bob Clowney. He took a fancy for Adeline's mammy, a bright 'latto gal slave on de place. White women in them days looked down on overseers as poor white trash. Him couldn't git a white wife but made de best of it by puttin' in his spare time a honeyin' 'round Adeline's mammy. Marse Bob stuck to him, and never 'jected to it.

"When de war come on, Marse Richard, de overseer, shoulder his gun as a soldier and, as him was educated more than most of de white folks, him rise to be captain in de Confederate Army. It's a pity him got kilt in dat war.

"My marster, Tom Dawkins, have a fine mansion, He owned all de land 'round Dawkins and had 'bout 200 slaves, dat lived in good houses and was we well fed. My pappy was de man dat run de mill and grind de wheat and corn into flour and meal. Him never work in de field. He was 'bove dat. Him 'tend to de ginnin' of de cotton and drive de carriage.

"De Yankees come and burn de mansion, de gin-house and de mill. They take all de sheep, mules, cows, hogs and even de chickens. Set de slaves free and us niggers have a hard time ever since.

"My black stepmammy was so mean to me dat I run away. I didn't know where to go but landed up, one night, at Adeline's mammy's and step-pappy's house, on Marse Bob Clowney's place. They had been slaves of Marse Bob and was livin' and workin' for him. I knock on de door. Mammy Charity, dat's Adeline's mammy, say: 'Who dat?' I say: 'Me'. Her say: 'Who is me?' I say: 'John'. Her say: 'John who?' I say: 'Just John'. Her say: 'Adeline, open de door, dat's just some poor boy dat's cold and hungry. Charity is my fust name. Your pappy ain't come yet but I'll let dat boy in 'til he come and see what he can do 'bout it.'

"When Adeline open dat door, I look her in de eyes. Her eyes melt towards me wid a look I never see befo' nor since. Mind you, I was just a boy fourteen, I 'spects, and her a woman twenty-five then. Her say: 'You darlin' little fellow; come right in to de fire.' Oh, my! She took on over me! Us wait 'til her pappy come in. Then him say: 'What us gonna do wid him?' Adeline say: 'Us gonna keep him.' Pappy say: 'Where he gonna sleep?' Adeline look funny. Mammy say: 'Us'll fix him a pallet by de fire.' Adeline clap her hands and say: 'You don't mind dat, does you boy?' I say: 'No ma'am, I is slept dat way many a time.'

"Well, I work for Marse Bob Clowney and stayed wid Adeline's folks two years. I sure made myself useful in dat family. Never 'spicioned what Adeline had in her head, 'til one day I climbed up a hickory nut tree, flail de nuts down, come down and was helpin' to pick them up when she bump her head 'ginst mine and say: 'Oh, Lordy!' Then I pat and rub her head and it come over me what was in dat head! Us went to de house and her told de folks dat us gwine to marry.

"Her led me to de altar dat nex' Sunday. Gived her name to de preacher as Adeline Cabean. I give de name of John Clowney Brown. Marse Bob was dere and laugh when de preacher call my name, 'John Clowney Brown.[']

"Our chillun come pretty fast. I was workin' for $45.00 a year, wid rations.

Us had three pounds of bacon, a peck of meal, two cups of flour, one quart of 'lasses, and one cup of salt, a week.

"Us never left Marse Robert as long as him lived. When us have four chillun, him increase de amount of flour to four cups and de 'lasses to two quarts. Then him built dis house for de old folks and Adeline and de chillun to live in. I help to build it forty-four years ago. Our chillun was Clarice, Jim, John, Charity, Tom, Richard, and Adeline.

"I followed Marse Robert Clowney in politics, wore a red shirt, and voted for him to go to de Legislature. Him was 'lected dat time but never cared for it no more.

"Adeline b'long to de church. Always after me to jine but I can't believe dere is anything to it, though I believes in de law and de Ten Commandments. Preacher calls me a infidel. Can't help it. They is maybe got me figured out wrong. I believes in a Great Spirit but, in my time, I is seen so many good dogs and hosses and so many mean niggers and white folks, dat I 'clare I is confused on de subject. Then I can't believe in a hell and everlastin' brimstone. I just think dat people is lak grains of corn; dere is some good grains and some rotten grains. De good grains is res'rected, de rotten grains never sprout again. Good people come up again and flourish in de green fields of Eden. Bad people no come up. Deir bodies and bones just make phosphate guano, 'round de roots of de ever bloomin' tree of life. They lie so much in dis world, maybe de Lord will just make 'lie' soap out of them. What you think else they would be fit for?"

Project #1655
W. W. Dixon
Winnsboro, S.C.

Thomas Campbell
Ex-Slave 82 Years Old.

[Six years old when the Civil War began, Campbell belonged to James McCants, a prominent Fairfield County lawyer. Since he never knew who his father was, this carriage driver with "skin as black as ink" considered his "white folks" his parents. He loyally wore the red shirt McCants gave him.]

"Good mornin' Marster Wood! Marster Donan McCants and Marster Wardlaw McCants both been tellin' me dat how you wants to see me but I's been so poorly and down at de heels, in my way of feelin', dat I just ain't of a mind or disposition to walk up dere to de town clock, where they say you want me to come. Take dis bench seat under de honey suckle vine. It shade you from de sun. It sho' is hot! I's surprise dat you take de walk down here to see a onery old man lak me.

"Yes sir, I was born, 'cordin' to de writin' in de Book, de 15th day of March, 1855, in de Horeb section of Fairfield District, a slave of ol['] Marster John Kennedy. How it was, I don't know. Things is a little mixed in my mind. Fust thing I 'members, and dreams 'bout sometimes yet, is bein' in Charleston, standin' on de battery, seein' a big ocean of water, wid ships and their white sails all 'bout, de waves leapin' and gleamin' 'bout de flanks of de ships in de bright sunshine, thousands of white birds flyin' 'round and sometimes lighting on de water. My mammy, her name Chanie, was a holdin' my hand and her other hand was on de handle of a baby carriage and in dat carriage was one of de Logan chillun. Whether us b'long to de Logans or whether us was just hired out to them I's unable to 'member dat. De slaves called him Marster Tom. Us come back to Fairfield in my fust childhood, to de Kennedy's.

"Marster John Kennedy raise more niggers than he have use for; sometime he sell them, sometime he hire them out. Him sell mammy and me to Marster James B. McCants and I been in de McCants family ever since, bless God!

"Marse James was a great lawyer in his day. I was his house boy and office boy. When I get older I take on, besides de blackin' of his boots and shoes and sweepin' out de office, de position of carriage driver and sweepin' out de church. Marster James was very 'ligious. Who my pa was? Dat has never been revealed to me. Thank God! I never had one, if they was lak I see nigger chillun have today. My white folks was all de parents I had and me wid a skin as black as ink. My belly was always full of what they had and I never suffer for clothes on my back or shoes on my feets.

"Does I 'members de Yankees? Yes sir, I 'member when they come. It was cold weather, February, now dat I think of it. Oh, de sights of them days. They camp all 'round up at Mt. Zion College and stable their hosses in one of de rooms. They gallop here and yonder and burn de 'Piscopal

Church on Sunday mornin'. A holy war they called it, but they and Wheeler's men was a holy terror to dis part of de world, as naked and hungry as they left it. I marry Savannah Parnell and of all our chillun, dere is just one left, a daughter, Izetta. Her in Tampa, Florida.

"Does I 'members anything 'bout de Ku Klux? No sir, nothin'. I was always wid de white folks side of politics. They wasn't concerned 'bout me. Marster James have no patience for dat kind of business anyhow. Him was a lawyer and believed in lettin' de law rule in de daylight and would have nothin' to do wid work dat have to have de cover of night and darkness.

"Does I 'member 'bout de red shirts? Sure I does. De marster never wore one. Him get me a red shirt and I wore it in Hampton days. What I recollect 'bout them times? If you got time to listen, I 'spect I can make anybody laugh 'bout what happen right in dis town in red shirt days. You say you glad to listen? Well, here goes. One time in '76.[,] de democrats have a big meetin' in de court house in April. Much talk last all day. What they say or do up dere nobody know. Paper come out next week callin' de radicals to meet in de court house fust Monday in May. Marster Glenn McCants, a lawyer, was one of old marster's sons. He tell me all 'bout it.

"De day of de radical republican meetin' in de court house, Marster Ed Ailen [Aiken] had a drug store, so him and Marster Ozmond Buchanan fix up four quart bottles of de finest kind of liquor, wid croton-oil in every bottle. Just befo' de meetin' was called to order, Marster Ed pass out dat liquor to de ring leader, tellin' him to take it in de court house and when they want to 'suade a nigger their way, take him in de side jury rooms and 'suade him wid a drink of fine liquor. When de meetin' got under way, de chairman 'pointed a doorkeeper to let nobody in and nobody out 'til de meetin' was over, widout de chairman say so.

"They say things went along smooth for a while but directly dat croton-oil make a demand for 'tention. Dere was a wild rush for de door. De doorkeeper say 'Stand back, you have to 'dress de chairman to git permission to git out'. Chairman rap his gavel and say 'What's de matter over dere? Take your seats! Parliment law 'quire you to 'dress de chair to git permission to leave de hall'. One old nigger, Andy Stewart, a ring leader, shouted: 'To hell wid Parliment law, I's got to git out of here.' Still de doorkeeper stood firm and faithful, as de boy on de burnin' deck, as Marster Glenn lak to tell it. One bright mulatto nigger, Jim Mobley, got out de tangle by movin' to take a recess for ten minutes, but befo' de motion could be carried out de croton-oil had done its work. Half de convention have to put on clean clothes and de court house steps have to be cleaned befo' they could walk up them again. You ask any old citizen 'bout it. Him will 'member it. Ask old Doctor Buchanan. His brother, de judge, was de one dat help Marster Ed Aiken to fix de croton-oil and whiskey.

"Well, dat seem to make you laugh and well it might, 'cause dat day been now long ago. Sixty-one years you say? How time gits along. Well, sixty-one years ago everybody laugh all day in Winnsboro, but Marster Ed never crack a smile, when them niggers run to his drug store and ask him for somethin' to ease their belly ache."

Project #1655
W. W. Dixon
Winnsboro, S.C.

Louisa Davis
Ex-Slave 106 Years Old.

[Before the Civil War, Sam Davis, a field hand, married Louisa Davis, a house servant to a wealthy planter family. Davis, who served as a body servant during the war, wore the red shirt in 1876, riding "long side of General Bratton." W. W. Dixon visited his widow, living in New Brookland (West Columbia). She recreated the paternalistic world they inhabited.]

"Well, well, well! You knows my white folks on Jackson Creek, up in Fairfield! I's mighty glad of dat, and glad to see you. My white folks comes to see me pretty often, though they lives way up dere. You wants to write me up? Well, I'll tell you all I recollect, and what I don't tell you, my daughter [, Plummy Glenn,] and de white folks can put in de other 'gredients. Take dis armchair and git dat smokin' ash tray; lay it on de window sill by you and make yourself comfortable and go ahead."

"I was born in de Catawba River section. My grandpappy was a full blood Indian; my pappy a half Indian; my mother, coal black woman. Just

Louisa Davis, widow of black Red Shirt Sam Davis, c. 1937. *Photo Collection, South Caroliniana Library, University of South Carolina.*

who I b'long to when a baby? I'll leave dat for de white folks to tell, but old Marster Jim Lemon buy us all; pappy, mammy, and three chillun: Jake, Sophie, and me[, all at once]. De white folks I fust b'long to refuse to sell 'less Marse Jim buy de whole family; dat was clever, wasn't it? Dis old Louisa must of come from good stock, all de way 'long from de beginnin', and I is sho' proud of dat."

"When he buy us, Marse Jim take us to his place on Little River nigh clean cross de county. In de course of time us fell to Marse Jim's son, John, and his wife, Miss Mary. [De white folks will tell you dat was in 1850.] I was a grown woman then and nursed their fust baby, Marse Robert. I see dat baby grow to be a man and 'lected to legislature, and stand up in dat Capitol over yonder cross de river [(You can see the Capitol from her front door in New Brookland)] and tell them de Law and how they should act, I did. They say I was a pretty gal, then, face shiny lak a ginger cake, and hair straight and black as a crow, and I ain't so bad to look at now, Marse Willie says."

"My pappy rise to be foreman on de place and was much trusted, but he plowed and worked just de same, mammy say maybe harder."

"Then one springtime de flowers git be blooming, de hens to cackling, and de guineas to patarocking. Sam come along when I was out in de yard wid de baby. He fust talk to de baby, and I asked him if de baby wasn't pretty. He say, 'Yes, but not as pretty as you is, Louisa.' I looks at Sam, and dat kind of foolishness wind up in a weddin'. De white folks allowed us to be married on de back piazza, and Reverend [Chalmers] Boggs performed de ceremony."

"My husband was a slave of de Sloans and didn't get to see me often as he wanted to; and of course, as de housemaid then, dere was times I couldn't meet him, clandestine like he want me. Us had some grief over dat, but he got a pass twice a week from his marster, Marse Tommie Sloan, to come to see me. Bold as Sam git to be, in after years ridin' wid a red shirt long side of General Bratton in '76, dat nigger was timid as a rabbit wid me when us fust git married. Shucks, let's talk 'bout something else. Sam was a field hand and drive de wagon way to Charleston once a year wid cotton, and always bring back something pretty for me."

"When de war come on, Sam went wid young Marster Tom Sloan as bodyguard, and attended to him and learned to steal chickens, geese, and turkeys for his young marster, just to tell 'bout it. He dead now; and what

I blames de white folks for, they never would give him a pension, though he spend so much of his time and labor in their service. I ain't bearin' down on my kind of white folks, for I'd jump wid joy if I could just git back into slavery and have de same white folks to serve and be wid them, day in and day out."

"Once a week I see de farm hands git rations at de smoke house, but dat didn't concern me. I was a housemaid and my mammy run de kitchen, and us got de same meals as my marster's folks did[, less de eggs and butter, what they didn't eat of them they sold]."

"Yes sir; I got 'possum. Know how to cook him now. Put him in a pot and parboil him, then put him in a oven wid lots of lard or fatback, and then bake him wid yaller yam potatoes, flanked round and round, and then wash him down wid locust and persimmon beer followed by a piece of pumpkin pie. Dat make de bestest meal I 'members in slavery days."

"Us got fish out of Little River nigh every Saturday, and they went good Sunday morning. Us had Saturday evenin's, dat is, de farm hands did, and then I got to go to see Sam some Sundays. His folks, de Sloans, give us a weddin' dinner on Sunday after us was married, and they sho' did tease Sam dat day."

"Like all rich buckra, de Lemons had hogs a plenty, big flock of sheep, cotton gin, slaves to card, slaves to spin, and slaves to weave. Us was well clothed and fed and 'tended to when sick. They was concerned 'bout our soul's salvation. Us went to church, learn de catechism; they was Presbyterians, and read de Bible to us. But I went wid Sam after freedom. He took de name of Davis, and I jined de Methodist Church and was baptized Louisa Davis."

"Patroller, you ask me? 'Spect I do member them. Wasn't I a good lookin' woman? Didn't Sam want to see me more than twice a week? Wouldn't he risk it widout de pass some time? Sure he did. De patrollers got after and run Sam many a time."

"After de war my pappy went to Florida. He look just like a Indian, hair and all, bushy head, straight and young lookin' wid no beard. We never heard from him since."

"De slaves wash de family clothes on Saturday and then rested after doin' dat. Us had a good time Christmas; every slave ketch white folks wid a holler, 'Christmas gift, Marster' and they holler it to each other. Us all hung our stockin's all 'bout de Big House, and then dere would be sumpin' in dere next mornin'. Lord, wasn't them good times!"

"Now how is it dese days? Young triflin' nigger boys and gals lyin' 'round puffin' cigarets, carryin' whiskey 'round wid them, and gittin' in jail on Christmas, grievin' de Lord and their pappies, and all sich things. Oh! De risin' generation and de future! What is it comin' to? I just don't know, but dere is comin' a time to all them."

"I sho' like to dance when I was younger. De fiddlers was Henry Copley and Buck Manigault; and if anybody 'round here could make a fiddle ring like Buck could, wouldn't surprise me none if my heart wouldn't cry out to my legs, 'Fust lady to de right and cheat or swing as you like, and on to de right'."

"Stop dat laughin'. De Indian blood in me have held me up over a hundred years, and de music might make me young again."

"Oh yes, us had ghost stories, make your hair stand on end, and us put iron in de fire when us hear screech owl, and put dream book under bed to keep off bad dreams."

"When de yankees come they took off all they couldn't eat or burn, but don't let's talk 'bout dat. Maybe if our folks had beat them and git up into dere country our folks would of done just like they did. Who knows?"

"You see dis new house, de flower pots, de dog out yonder, de cat in de sun lyin' in de chair on de porch, de seven tubs under de shed, de two big wash pots, you see de pictures hangin' round de wall, de nice beds, all dese things is de blessin's of de Lord through President Roosevelt. My grandson, Pinckney, is a World War man, and he got in de CCC Camp, still in it in North Carolina. When he got his bonus, he come down, and say, 'Grandma, you too old to walk, supposin' I git you a automobile?' I allow, 'Son, de Indian blood rather make me want a house.' Then us laugh. 'Well,' he say, 'Dis money I has and am continuin' to make, I wants you and mama to enjoy it.' Then he laugh fit to kill heself. Then I say, 'I been dreamin' of a tepee all our own, all my lifetime; buy us a lot over in Sugartown in New Brookland, and make a home of happiness for your ma, me and you'."

"And dis is de tepee you settin' in today. I feel like he's a young warrior, loyal and brave, off in de forests workin' for his chief, Mr. Roosevelt, and dat his dreams are 'bout me maybe some night wid de winds blownin' over dat three C camp where he is."

Project 1885–1
Folklore
Spartanburg—Dist.4
Edited by Elmer Turnage
May 18, 1937

Stories from Ex-Slaves [Pen Eubanks]

[A child during the Civil War, Eubanks remembered the excitement of serving as the flag bearer of a white Red Shirt club in Union county. The group met at a prominent local white Baptist church. Eubanks was proud of his role in electing Wade Hampton.]

"White folks, I sho nuff did ride wid de 'Red Shirts' fer Marse Hampton. Dar was two other darkies what rid wid us. Dey is bof daed now. One was Jack Jones, and de t'othern I does not recollect his name. Ham and Jack is both daed. Dat leave me de onliest living one what rid in de company.

"I rid in de company wid Marse Jimmie Young and he was de Cap'un. He live out yonder at Sardis Church. Ev'ybody know Marse Jimmie. He ain't quite as aged yet as I bees. Mr. J.T. Sexton, he rid from up around Cross Keys. He got de 'hole in de wall' and I calls on him yit, and us talks over de olden days. Miss Bobo's husband, he rid in Marse Jimmie's company. (Mr. Preston B. Bobo) Our company camped at de ole Brick church out whar de mansion set now. It has allus been called de Lower Fairforest Baptist Church, whar de white folks still goes, 'cept de done move de church down on de new road, further from de mansion and de ole graveyard. I lows dat you knows I is speaking o' de new mansion—Mr. Emslie Nicholson's house on de forest at de Shoals. I is got memory, but I ain't got no larning; dat I is proud of, kaise I is seed folks wid larning dat never knowed nothing worth speaking about. All de way 'fru', I is done tuck and stuck to my white folks—de Democratic white folks, dat I is.

"Sho was a pretty sight to see 'bout a hun'ded mens up on fine horses wid red shirts on. I still sees dem in my mind clear as day. Our red shirts fastened wid a strong band 'round de waist. Dar wasn't nar'y speck o' white to be seed no whars on 'em. Dey was real heavy and strong. Fact, dey was made from red flannel, and I means it was sho 'nough flannel, too. I had done kept one o' mine here till times got hard and den I tuck and tore it up fer me a undershirt, here past it been two winters when it got so cold.

"One night us set up all night and kept a big fire. Next morning it was de biggest frost all over de ground; but us never got one mite cold. De good white ladies of de community made our red shirts for us. I 'spects Marse Jimmie ken name some fer you.

"I got eve'y registration ticket in my house, and I still votes allus de democratic ticket. I has longed to de Democratic club ever since de red shirt days and I has voted dat way all de time. I was jes' turn't seventeen when I jined de Red Shirts and got into de Democratic Club, and I has been in it ever since. It ain't gwine out neither.

"I sho seed Hampton speak from Dr. Culp's porch. I voted fer him. At dat time, I lived on de Keenan place. Marse Jimmie Young, he de overseer for Mr. Keenan. Mr. Charles Ray owns and lives on it now. Dat brick church straight up de road from de Keenan place; straight as a bee line. Dat whar us met most o' de time fer de Red Shirt gatherings. Our Red Shirt Club was called de 'Fairforest' club atter de Lower Fairforest white folks Baptist church. De church has allus sot on de banks o' Fairforest Creek. Atter us got organized, I used to tote our flag. I was de onliest darky dat toted it.

"I is done handed you a few names; dey is all Democratic names. Lots of dem 'scapes my knowledge, it has all been so long ago. Dar was Mr. Gilmer Greer. Miss Gilmer Blankenship what lives out dar, she his niece. Mr. John Sims 'nother white man I members. Dar was lots o' companies in dis county, but I does not recall how many.

"Captain Jimmie Young would allus notify when dar was to be a meeting. Us darkies dat 'longed 'ud go and tell de white mens to come to de church. Us met sometime right 'fo de 'lection and all de companies come together at de ole courthouse dat stood right whar de new one is now.

"Robinson's Circus come to Union. De circus folks gib everbody a free ticket to de circus dat 'longed to de Democratic Club. Dey let all de scalawag niggers in fer registration tickets dat de Republicans had done give dem to vote fer Chamberlain. Dem niggers wanted to go to de circus wu'se dan dey wanted to do anything else. Dey never dre'mt dat dey was not a going to git to vote like de carpetbaggers, and de scalawags had done tole dem to do. Fact is, dey never much cared jes' since de got in de circus. Dem dat wanted de registration tickets back when de come out, never seed nobody to git 'em from nohows. Robinson's Circus was so big dat dey never showed it all in Union, but what dey had was out on McClure's field. It wasn't no houses dar den, and, o' course, dar wasn't no mill no whar about Union in dem days. All de tents dat was staked was staked in McClure's ole field over on 'Tosch' Branch. In dem days, dat field was de biggest territory in de clear around Union. Atter dat, all de Red Shirts met on de facade in front o' de courthouse. Mos' all de mens made a speech. Another darky sung a song like dis: 'Marse Hampton was a honest man; Mr. Chamberlain was a rogue'—Den I sung a song like dis: 'Marse Hampton et de watermelon, Mr. Chambeerlian knawed de rine.' Us jest having fun den, kaise us had done 'lected Marse Hampton as de new governor of South Ca'linia."

Source: "Uncle Pen" Eubanks, Hampton Ave. Union, S.C. (age 83)
Interviewer: Caldwell Sims, Union, S.C. (5/4/37)

Project 1885–1
Folklore
Spartanburg, Dist.4
Prepared by Elmer Turnage
Nov. 3, 1937

Stories from Ex-Slaves
[George Fleming]

[This field hand was born in 1854 on a large plantation in Laurens County. His narrative suggests that psychological factors shaped his decision to become a Red Shirt. Although his Republican father was murdered by Democrats in 1870, Fleming recalled being part of a Red Shirt group that killed the man in 1876. Considering his father "bullheaded," Fleming identified with his former master by voting for Wade Hampton.]

George Fleming and his wife, Elizabeth, live in a small two-room cottage at 349 Highland Street in Spartanburg, S.C. Their humble abode is typical of the average negro dwelling in this city. It is furnished with only the bare necessities compatible with comfortable living; but to George and Elizabeth it holds the same warmth and feeling of security which their idea of a home depicts. George has a keen memory and he talked freely of slavery.

"I was born in 1854 in de month of August. I disremembers what dat pension lady said was de day. She de one dat found out all about it. I 'clar dat was de biggest plantation whar I was born dat I is ever seed or heard tell of. Lawd a-mercy! Ain't no telling how many acres in dat place, but dar was jes' miles and miles of it. It was in Laurens County, not fur (far) from de town of Laurens. I 'longed to Marse Sam Fleming. Lawd chile, dat's de best white man what ever breathed de good air. I still goes to see whar he buried every time I gits a chance to venture t'wards Laurens. As old as I is, I still draps a tear when I sees his grave, fer he sho was good to me and all his other niggers.

"Marse Sam's boys, Lyntt and Frank, sho was tigers, but cose dey wasn't mean tigers. Dey had real long beards. Marse Lyntt was my young marster, and he de bestest man I ever know'd, 'cepting his daddy. He allus doing something to have fun outen us lil' niggers; but us didn't mind, 'cause we got fun outen it, too. I 'member how he used to sot us in de hog pens, but we wasn't scared as we 'lowed we was.

"My pa named Bill. He was stole from Virginia. I don't know how Marse got him. Sometimes dey would buy 'em and agin dey would steal 'em, sort of like stealing a dog. Ma, her name Hannah. Dey got married on de planatation. After pa got kil't, ma married a man called Charles. I only has one whole sister living, and she name Jennie. Viney and Millie be dead. My brother, Richard, he dead, too. My half-sister, Sallie Ann, she stay in Jacksonville, or some fureign state.

"Mercy on us, dem was de happy days; dey was heavenly days 'sides what we 'speriences now. Us lil' kids played lots of games den, some of dem like what dey plays now, but we had a better time. Befo' we was big enough to work, 'cept tote water and de like of dat, we played sech things as marbles. We had purty red and blue marbles dat Marse Lyntt brung frum de store. Sometimes we wrestle, too, and old Marse laugh till his fat belly shake all over when he see de lil' nigger's head buried in de white sand. Sometimes we play 'warm jacket'. Dat was worked by each one gitting a brush frum a tree or bush and frailing de other'un till it got too hot fer him.

"De older boys and gals had big frolics, 'specially in de fall of de year. Sometimes dey be on our plantation, and agin dey be on neighboring ones.

When dey have 'em close home, some of us lil' niggers would slip off and git in de corner or up in de loft of de house and spy on 'em. Dey cotch us sometimes and thrash us out. One game dey played was 'please and dis-please'. When de gal say, 'What it take to please you?' de boy say, 'A kiss frum dat purty gal over dar'. Yes, dey played 'hack-back', too. Dat's when dey faced each other and trotted back and forth. Lawd, dey sho had some awful times dancing and cutting jigs. Twan't much drinking, 'cepting on de side.

"White ladies didn't go to de frolics, but some of de white men did. De patrollers was allus around to see dat everybody had passes, and if dey didn't have 'em dey was run back home. Sometimes de overseer was dar, too. Lawd, dey sho did kick up de dust at dem frolics. De music was mostly made by fiddles, and sometimes dey had quill blowers. De quills was made frum cane, same as de spindles was but dey was cut longer and was different sizes. All de quills was put in a rack and you could blow any note you wanted to off of dem. Boy, I sho could blow you out of dar wid a rack of quills. I was de best quill blower dat ever put one in a man's mouth. I could make a man put his fiddle up; hit you so hard wid Dixieland dat I knock you off de seat. Gals wouldn't look at nobody else when I start blowing de quills.

"Dar was also heaps and lots of other big affairs 'sides de frolics. De cornshuckings—Lawd a-mercy, you ain't seen nothing. Niggers frum all over de place shucking corn and somebody setting on one of de big piles calling de cornshucking song, jes' like dey do in de square dance. Dat kept 'em happy—everybody jine in de chorus. A jug of liquor sot at de bottom of de pile; everybody try to be first to get to de liquor. Lawd, dey holler and take on something awful when dey get to de bottom. White folks have big supper ready; liquor, brandy and everything. Dem was de times; pick up somebody and kivver 'em up wid de shucks. Had cotton pickings, too. Dat work not so fast but we had good times. Sometimes dey be on our plantation; den we sometimes go to other places.

"Didn't need no passes when a bunch of slaves went to other plantations to dem big gatherings. 'Rangements was already made so de patrollers wouldn't bother nobody. Dat policy didn't hold fer de frolics, though. Sho had to have a pass frum de marse if you went.

"On de plantation we lived jes' like a great big family wid Marse de daddy of 'em all. Cose he had overseers to watch atter de work and keep things straight. He allus kept more dan 200 head of slaves. De quarters was made up of lots of cabins, some wid one room, some wid two or three. Dat's 'cording to how big de family was. Dey wasn't built in rows, but scattered about over de planatation. Some of de cabins was made of logs and some wid planks, but all was warm and comfortable. Dey had all kinds of chimneys, too. Some brick, some rock and some de old stick and mud kind. Dey all had big fireplaces. Dat was whar us done de cooking. Hitches (hooks) was on de sides of de fireplace whar big iron pots hung to bile and cook in. We had pans and leads (lids) and things to bake in, too. Yes Lawd, dem was de days, fer we sho had plenty to eat—everything we wanted.

"All de things we had in de house was home-made, but we sho had good beds. Dey made wid boards, and 'stead of slats, ropes was stretched twixt de sides real tight by slipping dem through holes and making knots in de ends. Over dese we laid bags; den feather or straw ticks. We had plenty kivvers to keep us warm. We had shelves and hooks to put our clothes on. We had benches and tables made wid smooth boards. Missus Harriet, dat Marse Sam's wife, she give us a looking-glass so we could see how to fix up. Lawd a-mercy, Missus Harriet was one fine woman. She allus looked atter us to see dat we didn't suffer fer nothing.

"Some of de women dat didn't have a passel of lil' brats was 'signed to de job of cooking fer de field hands. Some of 'em come home to eat, but mostly dey stayed in de fields. De dinner horn blow'd 'zactly at 12 o'clock and dey know'd it was time fer grub. Everybody drapped what dey was doing and compiled demselves in groups. Dey could see de buckets coming over de hill. Dar was more dan one group, fer de fields was so big dat dey couldn't all come to one place. Cose all dat was planned out by de overseers. Had lots of overseers and dey had certain groups to look out fer.

"Most of de food was brung to de fields in buckets, but sometimes de beans and de like of dat come in de same pots dey was cooked in. It took two big niggers to tote de big pots. Dar was no want of food fer de hands. Marse know'd if dey worked dey had to eat. Dey had collards, turnips and other good vegetables wid cornbread. Chunks of meat was wid de greens, too, and us had lots of buttermilk.

"Women worked in de field same as de men. Some of dem plowed jes' like de men and boys. Couldn't tell 'em apart in de field, as dey wore pantelets or breeches. Dey tied strings 'round de bottom of de legs so de loose dirt wouldn't git in deir shoes. De horn blow'd to start work and to quit. In de morning when de signal blow'd, dey all tried to see who could git to de field first. Dey had a good time and dey liked to do deir work. Us didn't pay much mind to de clock. We worked frum sun to sun. All de slaves had to keep on de job, but dey didn't have to work so hard. Marse allus said dey could do better and last longer by keeping 'em steady and not over-working 'em.

"Dar was all kinds of work 'sides de field work dat went on all de time. Everybody had de work dat he could do de best. My daddy worked wid leather. He was de best harness maker on de place, and he could make shoes. Dey had a place whar dey tanned cow-hides. Dat was called de tannos. Dey didn't do much spinning and weaving in de home quarters; most of it was done in one special place Marse had made fer dat purpose. Some of de slaves didn't do nothing but spin and weave, and dey sho was good at it, too. Dey was trained up jes' fer dat particular work.

"I don't know how many spinning wheels and looms and dem things Marse had, but he sho had lots of 'em. Dat business making cloth had lots to it and I don't know much 'bout it, but it was sort of dis way. Dey picked de seeds out of de cotton; den put de cotton in piles and carded it. Dey kept brushing it over and over on de cards till it was in lil' rolls. It was den ready fer de spinning wheels whar it was spun in thread. Dis was called de filling. I don't know much 'bout de warp, dat is de part dat run long ways.

"Dem spinning wheels sho did go on de fly. Dey connected up wid de spindle and it go lots faster dan de wheel. Dey hold one end of de cotton roll wid de hand and 'tach de other to de spindle. It keep drawing and twisting de roll till it make a small thread. Sometimes dey would run de thread frum de spindle to a cornshuck or anything dat would serve de purpose. Dat was called de broach. Some of dem didn't go any further dan dat, dey had to make sech and sech broaches a day. Dis was deir task. Dat's de reason some of dem had to work atter dark, dat is, if dey didn't git de task done befo' dat.

"Dey run de thread off de broach on to reels, and some of it was dyed on de reels. Dey made deir own dyes, too. Some of it was made frum copperas, and some frum barks and berries. Atter while, de thread was put back on de spinning wheel and wound on lil' old cane quills. It was den ready fer de looms. Don't know nothing, de looms—boom! boom! sho could travel. Dey put de quills, atter de thread was wound on dem, in de shettle and knocked it back and forth twixt de long threads what was on de beams. Can't see de thread fly out of dat shettle it come so fast. Dey sho could sheckle it through dar. Dey peddled dem looms, zip! zap! making de thread rise and drap while de shettle zoom twixt it. Hear dem looms booming all day long 'round de weaving shop. De weaving and spinning was done in de same place.

"Overseers lived on de plantation. No, dey wasn't poor whites. All Marse Sam's overseers was good men. Dey lived wid deir families, and Marse's folks 'sociated wid dem, too. Dey had good houses to live in. Dey built better dan ours was. Marse didn't 'low dem to whip de slaves, but dey made us keep straight. If any whipping had to be done, Marse done it, but he didn't have to do much. He didn't hurt 'em bad, den, jes' git a big hick'ry and lay on a few. He would say if dat nigger didn't walk de chalk, he would put him on de block and settle him. Dat was usually enough, 'cause Marse mean't dat thing and all de niggers know'd it.

"Jes' one or two of Marse Sam's slaves ever run away, but lots of other niggers did. Some of dem try to go to de North, but mostly dey come polling back by demselves when dey git hungry. If dey didn't come back purty soon, deir marse sont out to look fer 'em. Lawd, I heard de nigger hounds yelping befo' day many times. Dat was de bloodhounds dey sicked on de runaway niggers, and dey sho run 'em back home. When dey hear de hounds dey was glad to git home.

"De patrollers would go out and look fer de niggers. Dey almost skin 'em alive if dey cotch 'em befo' dey git home. Patrollers was made up of jes' anybody dat wanted to jine 'em, poor white trash and all. One thing dey sho couldn't do, and dat was tech a nigger atter he done got on his marse's grounds. Dey almost got pa one time, but he saved his hide by falling over a rail fence jes' befo' dey cotched him. All de plantation owners, dey pay so much to de patrollers to be on de look-out fer de slaves, and dat's de way dey kept so many frum running away.

"Some men, like old Joe Crews, was reg'lar nigger traders. Dey bought niggers, stole 'em frum Virginia and places and drove 'em through de country like a bunch of hogs. Dey come in great gangs. In town dey have big nigger sellings, and all de marsters frum all over de countryside be dar to bid on 'em. Dey put 'em up on de block and holler 'bout dis and dat dey could do and how strong dey was. 'Six hundred—Yip, Yip, make it six-fifty' I heard 'em call many times when I be dar wid Marse. Some of dem throw a thousand dollars quick as dey would ten at a purty gal. Some traders stop a drove of niggers at de plantation and swap or sell some. Dey didn't call dat putting 'em on de block like when day had de big selling.

"Slaves started to work by de time dey was old enough to tote water and pick up chips to start fires wid. Some of dem started to work in de fields when dey about ten, but most of 'em was older. Lawd, Marse Sam must have had more dan a dozen house niggers. It took a lot of work to keep things in and 'round de house in good shape. Cose most of de slaves was jes' field hands, but some of dem was picked out fer special duties. Slaves didn't get any pay in money fer work, but Marse give 'em a lil' change sometimes.

"Everybody have plenty to eat. Lots of times we had fish, rabbits, possums and stuff like dat; lots of fishing and hunting in dem days. Some slaves have lil' gardens of deir own, but most de vegetables come frum de big garden. Missus was in charge de big garden, but cose she didn't have to do no work. She sho seed atter us too. Even de poor white trash had plenty to eat back in dem times. Marse have a hundred head of hogs in de smokehouse at one time. Never seen so much pork in my life. We sho lived in fine fashion in hog killing time, cose de meats was cured and us had some all de year. Yes sir, Marse ration out everybody some every week. Watermelons grow awful big, some of 'em weigh a hundred pounds. Dey big striped ones, called 'rattlesnakes', so big you can't tote it no piece. All de baking and biling was done over de big fireplaces.

"Didn't wear much clothes in summer 'cause we didn't need much, but all de grown niggers had shoes. Lawd, I wore many pair of Marse Lyntt's boots, I means sho 'nuff good boots. Marse had his own shoemakers, so twan't no use us gwine widout. Had better clothes fer Sunday. Most de washing was done on Saturday afternoons, and we be all setting purty fer Sunday. Cold weather we was dressed warm, and we had plenty bed kivvers, too. Cose all slaves didn't have it as good as Marse Sam's did. Lawd, I is seed lil' naked niggers setting on de rail fences like pa'cel of buzzards; but Marse Sam's niggers never had to go dat way.

"Slaves didn't have no church or schools. Lots of dem went to de white folks' church, but Marse Sam didn't make his slaves go if dey didn't want to. Deir benches was on de sides and in de back of de church. All preachers was white men. Old preacher Moore sho was a humdinger, and a good one. He pizen deir minds wid Salvation, soak 'em in de oil of Holy Ghost and set 'em on fire. Lawd-a-me! When he got lit up all over till his eyes shine and sparkle, he sho could bring down de house. Twan't no seats in school fer de slaves, though. Some of de slick ones slipped around and larn't de letters.

"When de slaves come frum de field, deir day's work was done. Fact is, everybody's work was done 'cept maybe some of de spinners or weavers dat didn't quite finish deir task. Dey was de onliest ones dat had to ever work atter dark, and dat not often. Sometimes on Saturdays we didn't have to work a-tall, dat is in de fields, and sometimes we had to work till 12 o'clock. Lots of de men went fishing and hunting, and mostly de women washed. Saturday nights some groups would git together and sing. I can still hear dem old songs in my mind, but I doesn't recalls de words. Christmas sho was handsome time. Christmas and New Years we had a good time. Marse jes' sort of turned 'em loose. We got a lil' extra liquor and brandy on de holidays, but cose we had some all along enduring de whole entire year. Marse had three stills on de place and dar was plenty liquor, but he didn't let anybody git drunk. He call de lil' niggers, too, sometimes and give 'em a drink, and he give 'em jelly biscuits. He call everybody up to de big house on Christmas and make a speech; den he give everybody some good brandy.

"I doesn't recalls nothing 'bout no ghosts. Ain't nothing in dem things. Cose if you goes 'round de graveyards atter dark, you might see sech things, but I ain't gwine dar. Nigger come in once a-telling something 'bout a witch making a knot in his horse's tail, but I don't think dar was nothing to it.

"When any of de slaves got sick, Marse took good care of 'em till dey got well. If dey bad sick he sont fer de doctor. Some of de women know'd how to bile up herbs and roots and make tea fer colds and fevors, but I don't know what kind dey used. When de chilluns was born, Marse seed to it dat de mammy was rightly took care of. He kept a old granny woman wid dem till dey got up and well.

"De slaves mostly got married in Marse Sam's back yard, and he sho fixed up fine fer 'em. Dat's de way ma and pa got married. I got married twice on Dr. Wright's place. He fixed up fer de 'casion like Marse did. Had twelve waiters both times. We had supper in de kitchen and den had dancing and music. Dem dat got married back den sho did have it in high fashion. Man would have a good striped suit, and de woman have silk and satin clothes. Dey was married by a white preacher same as de white folks. A dinner was fixed in deir honor, too. Cose, as I say, Marse Sam's slaves was treated better dan most any I ever know'd of, and all of dem loved him, too.

"Dar was a burying ground jes' fer de slaves and de funeral was sort of like dat of de white folks. Niggers was baptized jes' like de white people, too, and by de same preacher. I saw thirty niggers baptized at one time in de river. Dat's whar everybody was baptized, den. Now dey has a basin in de church, wid glass all 'round de top, but I 'spects it do 'bout as much good.

"During de war, food got kind of scace but didn't nobody suffer none on our place. Lawd yes, we carried de farming right on while de war was gwine one. Marse Sam's boys went to de war, but dey come back all right. Dey sho had a home-coming time fer 'em when dey got back. I heard 'bout de Yankees coming through and 'stroying things, but I never seed none. Our place stood jes' like it was all enduring de war. I didn't see no Ku Klux, neither. When freedom come, Marse called all de slaves up to de big house and say, 'I wants to know what you all is gwine to do now, fer you is free to go if you wants to.' Everybody spoke alike, 'We wants to stay wid Marse.' Everyone of de slaves stayed right on wid Marse Sam till dey could git a place to go to. Lots of 'em stayed till dey died. He divided de land up in patches and give each one a third of what was made.

"Soon atter de war dar was a lot of trouble 'bout voting fer de governor. Folks like old Joe Crews tried to put in de niggers' heads to vote fer de Republicans, but I know'd better. I voted fer Hampton like Marse did. Fact is, I voted twice fer him. Joe Crews, and other scalawags like him, had done made all de money dey could off selling niggers, so dey thought dey could make some more by making 'greements wid de Republicans. My daddy, Bill, was bullheaded. He done got dem ideas in his head and he said he gwine to vote fer de Republicans in spite of hell.

"De Democrats done got scared 'cause so many niggers gwine to vote fer de other side, so dey formed a s'ciety called de Red Shirts. Dat was jes' to scare de niggers frum coming to de polls. I was young, but I jined right up wid dem and wore a red shirt, too.

"Dey had a reg'lar battle in Laurens when de voting started. All de Republican niggers had deir guns stored in Tin Pot Alley, fer Joe Crews told 'em dey couldn't bring 'em to de polls. He thought de Yankees would protect de niggers, but fact is, de Yankees done been paid off by de Democrats and left town. Us Democrats broke in de storehouse in Tin Pot Alley and got every one of dem guns. De niggers names was on de stock of de guns. We sho had a hot time when dem niggers come up dar trying to vote. Dat's when my daddy got kil't. He had already been shot in de leg befo' dat, and dey called him 'cripple Bill'. Dem was de purtiest guns I ever seed. Dey blick three times when de trigger was pulled back. Old Jim Crews was kil't, too, at dat time. Wash Hill was de one dat got him. He was shot at Crew's Branch. Twan't long atter dat till things begin to settle down, fer de Democrats sho did lick up dem Republlicans.

"I been marred three times, first time I married Sarah Peterson. I 'clar to goodness I sho can't 'member dat second one. Let me see, let me see—Lonie, Lonie, oh yes, Lonie Golding. Us married in Larens County on Dr. Wright's place whar I married de first one. She didn't live long and we didn't have no chilluns. My last wife name Elizabeth McKantz, she frum Abbeville. She cooked fer Mr. Jones. Her daddy was a white man, and she look jes' like a Indian. I jes' had one chile by de first wife, but he dead. His name was Richard. I got two chilluns by de last wife dat be living. Dat's Mattie, de oldest, and Hugh, de third one. I doesn't know whar neither one lives now. My other two dat's dead was Anna and George Anna. Yes, dey both named Anna, but de first one dead befo' de other one was born.

"Some folks didn't like slavery, but I sho did. Mercy Lawd, we had a good time, den; heap better dan now. I been a long time gitting dis pension, and it ain't much when you gits it. Back in slavery times we didn't have no worries 'bout rent or something to eat. We had a job long as we lived, dat is if freedom hadn't come."

Source: George Fleming (83), 349 Highland St, Spartanburg, S.C.
Interviewer: Elmer Turnage, Dist.4 office, Spartanburg, S.C.
Oct. 28, 1937.

Project 1885–1
Folklore
Spartanburg Dist. 4
Edited by Elmer Turnage
June 22, 1937

Stories from Ex-Slaves [Madison Griffin]

[Eight years old at the outbreak of the Civil War, Griffin was a farm laborer in Newberry County in 1880. Recalling the harshness of slavery and the violence of the Ku Klux Klan, he opted to support Wade Hampton.]

"I will be 85 years old dis coming August. My master said I was 14 years old de August coming after freedom.

"My master was Billy Scott who had seven or eight hundred acres of land, and 48 slaves. He wouldn't have no white overseers, but had some nigger foremen dat sometimes whipped de niggers, and de master would whip dem, too. He was a fair man, not so good and not so mean. He give us poor quarters to live in, and sometimes plenty to eat, but sometimes we went hungry. He had a big garden, plenty cows, hogs and sheep. De most we had ter eat, was corn, collards, peas, turnip-greens and home-made molasses. We had wheat bread on Sundays. It was made from flour grind at our own mill. We didn't have but one day off, that was Christmas Day and den we had to grind our axes.

"We made our clothes out of cotton and wool mixed, made dem at home wid our own cards and spinning wheels. We made our shoes out of leather tanned at home, but had to use woolen shoes after de war, which would wear out and split open in three weeks.

"My daddy was Amos Wilson and mammy was Carline Griffin. I had some brothers and sisters. When freedom come, de master come to us and told us de damn Yankees done freed us, 'what you gwinter do? If you want ter stay on wid me, I will give you work.' We stayed fer awhile.

"The patrollers caught me once when I run off. I run fast and lost my hat and dey got it. I saw some slaves sold on de block. Dey was put in a ring and sold by crying out de price. We didn't learn to read and write, not allowed to. De niggers went to de corn shuckings and was give pumpkin custards to eat and liquor. Dey wasn't allowed to dance, but sometimes we had secret dances, shut up in de house so de master couldn't hear us.

"After de war, we went hunting and fishing on Sundays. We never had Saturday afternoons off. We killed wild deer and other things. Once de master killed 14 squirrels in three quarters of hour.

"We raised our own tobacco, the master did, for home use. Most always a small patch was planted.

"De master once saw ghosts, he come from his sisters and passed de graveyard and saw 9 cows with no heads. His horse jest flew home. Most white folks didn't believe in ghosts, but dat is one time de master believed he saw some.

"I went wid de Red Shirts, belonged to de company and went to meetings wid dem. I voted for Hampton. Befo' dat, de Ku Klux had bad niggers dodging like birds in de woods. Dey caught some and threw dem on de ground and whipped dem, but de master say he don't know nothing 'bout it as he was asleep. Dey caught a nigger preacher once and made him dance, put him in muddy water and walloped him around in de mud.

"Once seven Indians come in our neighborhood and call fer meat, meal and salt. Dere was three men and four women. Dey cooked all night, murmuring something all de time. Next morning three squirrels was found up a tree, and de Indians shot 'em down wid bow and arrow.

"One time I saw horses froze to death. Dey couldn't get dere breath, and de people took warm water and wash dere foreheads. I was a small boy den. My master had 46 guineas.

"I married Nancy Robinson who belonged to Robert Calmes. She was living at de Gillam place near Rich Hill.

"We used to ask a riddle like this: Love I stand, Love I sit, Love I hold in my right hand. What is it? It was made up when an old woman had a little dog named 'Love'. She killed it and put a part of it, after it was baked, in her stockings; part in her shoes; part in back of her dress, and part in her gloves. A nigger was going to be hung the next Friday, and told if he guess the riddle he would be turned loose. He couldn't guess it, but was turned loose any way.

"I think Abe Lincoln might ter done good, but he had us all scared to death, took our mules and burned our places. Don't know anything about Jeff Davis. Booker Washington is all right.

"I joined de church when 28 years old, because I thought it was right. Wanted to git right and git to God's Kingdom. I think everybody ought to join de church.

"O' course I rather it not be slavery time, but I got more ter eat den dan now. Den we didn't know what ter do, but now we perish ter death."

Source: Madison Griffin (84), Whitmire, S.C.
Interviewer: G. L. Summer, Newberry, S.C. (6/18/1937)

Project #–1655
Folklore
Charleston, S.C.
Martha S. Pinckney
Approx. 1050 words

Richard Mack
Ex-Slave 104 Years Old

[Born in Virginia in 1833, Mack came to Orangeburg County, South Carolina, before the Civil War. As a Confederate body servant, he genuinely bonded with the officers he served. After the war, he stumped the state with General Hampton.]

Richard Mack, a happy philosopher, 104 years old, in perfect mental and physical condition, is still working as janitor of the Rosemont school. He is of the aquiline type, with eyes bright and deep set, and a black skin with a red light shining through, showing Indian relationship.

"I was born in Limestone, Va. My first master was Green Bobo. I was sold when I was ten years old; not really sold, but sold on a paper that said if he didn't take care of me, I would come back—a paper on me—a kind of mortgage—speculators bought negroes and sell um. Missis, I never had a stripe put on me. I had a privilege of being among all people. (Richard Mack enjoyed every experience of his life and has no root of bitterness in his nature). Then I come to South Carolina. My mother, Jane, she live to be 108; she come to South Carolina too. We got back together again (he paused with a bright smile) Orangeburg, at Captain Cherry's—Captain Cherry here in Charleston is related to him—Cherry Plantation is there now; Captain Cherry had plenty of money."

"Tony was my father, a carriage driver; he wore his tall hat and fine clothes (livery) and he was a musician—played the violin at the Academy on the 'old Ninety-Six Road'. All the white people educated their children there, and they had parties. Oh, the beautifulest ladies—they wore long dresses then and had long hair—the beautifulest! My father—Daddy Tony, they call him—he was a musician—always played the violin." Here he mentioned the names of songs of that day, before the War of 1861, and repeated these words with such merriment:

> "Would have been married forty year ago,
> If it hadn't been for Cotton Eye Joe"
> "Songs—lots of um—
> "Run, nigger, run, de *Patrol ketch* you"

He roared with laughter—"When de patrol come, I had my badge; I show him my paper and my badge! I got it still. I love dem days—I love dem people."

"My mother was a good woman—she used to get down on her knees, like this, and get up like this" (he knelt with agility, and rose unassisted, quickly, and without the least difficulty). ["] My aunt lived to be 141; she saw George Washington—she told me so."

"Cherokee—kickapoo—I don't remember—my great grandfather was an Indian Chief—my nose is straight, see here." He went into the pocket of his overall brought out a pair of eyeglasses, put them on the end of his nose, and looked over them.

"I loved dem days, I loved dem people. We lived better—we had no money—we had nothing to worry about—just do your task. Spin wheel and reel and reel for the yarn. I filled my arms full of quilt—hand made. Had task; I done all my task, and I help others with their task so they wouldn't get whipped; if people lazy and wont do, they got to be made to do; if children bad they get whipped—if nigger bad, they get a whipping."

"Old Satan wear a big shoe—he got one club foot. He can disguise himself—he make you think he got power, but he ain't got any power. He get you in trouble and leave you there. I always pray for wisdom and understanding like Solomon. I pray all the time to our good Father. People say—'Why you call him Good Father?' (Quoted from the Bible) I love everybody—'Love thy neighbor as thyself.'

"Yes Ma'am! Oh Heaven!—we got to be clean—we change out of the flesh to the spirit; a crown prepared for us; all we save and help are stars in our crown; you go from Mansion to Mansion—higher—higher." (He raised his arms with a rapt look)

Then he was told about "Green Pastures" and asked what he thought of it. "Why my Lord have Mercy! The Lord is a Spirit—we are changed."

"I roll the carpet for Missis to get in the carriage; a two-feet carpet from the house roll to the stoop for the carriage."

"My mother—yes Ma'am—108 years old—a smart woman in the house. Oh my Lord, Missis—cook! She wouldn't kill a chicken out of the yard; she had a coop to put them in, and it was cleaned out every day. My mother would fix the flowers; she would take this little flower, and that little flower, and put them together, and make up a beautiful bouquet, and hand them out to everybody. My father knew all about planting; the people would come to ask 'Daddy Tony' how to plant this and when to plant that."

"I heard all the War talk, I saw a comet." (Indicating its position in the heavens, he seemed inspired, forgot his surroundings, looking back). "I saw the curtain-cloud—and snow clouds—rolls and rolls. In the War I was with my master, Capt. Cherry, and Dr. Knox, Captain in the Civil War, and Capt. Dick McMichael—all those fine gentlemen. They had hog-skin saddles that creaked—Crench—crench—as they rode; (He was enthusiastic) the way they could ride! Those hosses were as sensible as people; they could jump from side to side; they knew everything."

"Capt. Cherry said to me—'Why weren't you white! Why weren't you white! Why weren't you white!' I lost my old Captain—then I was with Gen. Frank Bamberg, and with his brother, Capt. Isaac Bamberg—I was Orderly. Sometimes in the War we had one hardtack a day, and had to drink water on 'um, to make 'um swell. We had to get out salt out of water, most anywhere."

"I saw Gen. Lee many times; I knew him; he had his close beard around his face; he looked fine and sat his horse so splendid." Mack was asked the color of the horse, and described the gray. Here he remembered the battlefield—"I did this"—he enacted silently—dexterously—the placing of the dead and wounded on the stretchers and bearing them away—worked so rapidly that his breath was labored. "I made the balloon flight—my eyes were good—they carried me because any object that I saw, I know what it was; a rope ladder led up to the basket—the beautiful thing—we went up on the other side of Beaufain street; there were no houses there then, and we came down on the Citadel Green."

Mack had spoken several times with enthusiasm of the officer's cavalry 'pump sole boots'. After he had polished them—"Capt. Edwards (of Elloree) gave me a $500.00 bill for cleaning his 'pump sole boots'." Mack proudly enacted the Captain's jolly but pompous manner, as he gave the bill, and added, "I had thousands of dollars *in* Confederate money when the War broke up. If we had won I would be rich."

After War period: "The time Capt. Wade Hampton was stumping I followed him all over the State; I led 500 head; was with him to Camden, Orangeburg and all the way to Hampton County; led 500 negroes through the County; I was Captain of then; I rode 'Nellie Ponsa' and wore my red jacket and cap and boots; I had a sword too; my 'red shirt' died year before last."

Asked if he knew 'Riley', Mack answered promptly—'Democract [Democrat] Riley', yes Ma'am, used to drive that fine carriage, and old Col. Cunningham's family." Riley was an ex-slave, a tall black man, devoted to the South, as he was, a Democrat of high principle, and respected by all—hated by many—a power in himself.

"I lose all my ancestors. I got a niece, Queenie Brown, in Orangeburg; I got a daughter in New Jersey; one in New York, married to a Clyde Line man; lost sight of both; both old."

"Bless the Lord! I got friends! Mr. Pooser came to see me yesterday; been in South America four years; just got back and hunt me up right off! Married Miss Dantzler of Orangeburg—I raised them all."—with a benign look of love and ownership.

Source: Richard Mack, Rosemont School, Charleston, S.C.

NOTES

Preface

1. For a post-revisionist overview of Reconstruction, see Eric Foner, *Reconstruction: America's Unfinished Revolution, 1862–1877* (New York: Harper and Row, 1989). See his bibliography for a listing of post-revisionist works.

2. Clarence E. Walker, *Deromanticizing Black History: Critical Essays and Reappraisals* (Knoxville: University of Tennessee Press, 1991), xviii. For black Confederates, see Richard Rollins, ed., *Black Southerners in Gray: Essays on Afro-Americans in Confederate Armies, Journal of Confederate History* Series, vol. 11 (Murfreesboro, Tenn.: Southern Heritage Press, 1994), and Ervin L. Jordan Jr., *Black Confederates and Afro-Yankees in Civil War Virginia* (Charlottesville: University Press of Virginia, 1995).

3. Walker, *Deromanticizing Black History,* xv.

4. For blacks as Southerners, see John B. Boles, *Black Southerners, 1619–1869* (Lexington: University Press of Kentucky, 1983), and Boles, ed., *Masters and Slaves in the House of the Lord: Race and Religion in the American South, 1740–1870* (Lexington: University Press of Kentucky, 1988). For a moving account of mistreatment of blacks by Sherman's soldiers in Columbia, see Charles Royster, *The Destructive War: William Tecumseh Sherman, Stonewall Jackson, and the Americans* (New York: Alfred A. Knopf, 1991), chap. 1. In *Been in the Storm So Long: The Aftermath of Slavery* (New York: Alfred A. Knopf, 1979), Leon F. Litwack noted how some blacks tended toward reconciliation with whites. See 551, 554–55.

5. *Abbeville Medium,* September 6, 20, 1876.

6. This summary of Reconstruction is based on Thomas Holt, *Black over White: Negro Political Leadership in South Carolina during Reconstruction* (Urbana: University of Illinois Press, 1979); Hampton M. Jarrell, *Wade Hampton and the Negro: The Road Not Taken* (Columbia: University of South Carolina Press, 1950); Francis Butler Simkins and Robert Hilliard Woody, *South Carolina during Reconstruction* (Chapel Hill: University of North Carolina Press, 1932); Joel Williamson, *After Slavery: The Negro in South Carolina during Reconstruction, 1861–1877* (Chapel Hill: University of North Carolina Press, 1965; reprint, Hanover, N.H.: University Press of New England, Wesleyan University Press, 1990).

7. The testimonies come from U.S. Congress, Senate, *South Carolina in 1876: Testimony as to the Denial of the Elective Franchise in South Carolina at the Elections of 1875 and 1876*, 44th Cong., 2d sess., S. Misc. Doc. 48 (Washington, D.C.: Government Printing Office, 1877) (hereafter cited as *South Carolina in 1876*).

The eleven slave narratives were collected by the Federal Writers' Project of the Works Progress Administration (hereafter cited as Slave Narratives). Ten are in the Manuscript Division of the Library of Congress, Washington, D.C. They are formally cataloged under United States Work Projects Administration (WPA) Collection, Federal Writers' Project: Slave Narrative Project, Slave Narratives, South Carolina, vol. 14, container A928, pt. 1 (Abrams-Durant), pt. 2 (Eddington-Hunter), and container A929, pt. 3 (Jackson-Quattlebaum), pt. 4 (Raines-Young). Each part was bound (part and page numbers will be cited). Container A907 includes unbound copies of the slave narratives in folders. It also has narratives not in the bound parts. Comments by WPA appraisers about the slave narratives, arranged chronologically by the surname of the interviewee, are in container A906 under South Carolina, Appraisal Sheets, "A-Y" (hereafter cited as Appraisal Sheets). George Fleming's narrative as well as copies of most of the others are available in the WPA Federal Writers' Project Papers, Ex-Slave Narratives, of the South Caroliniana Library, University of South Carolina, Columbia. Also see George P. Rawick, ed., *The American Slave: A Composite Autobiography* (Westport, Conn.: Greenwood Publishing Co., 1972, 1977), vol. 2, pts. 1, 2; vol. 3, pts. 3, 4; Supplement, Series 1, vol. 11.

The documents have been reproduced as is with the following exceptions. Obvious typing mistakes have been corrected in brackets. Corrections by the typist or supervisory editor have been made without duplicating the insertion or deletion marks. A space has been inserted to divide words that run together. In two instances the names of the persons interviewed have been placed at the beginning in brackets. At least in three cases, brackets in the original testimonies have been replaced by parentheses to distinguish the material from editorial emendation.

Students of the slave narratives should consider viewing the material available at the state level. Some of the slave narratives at the South Caroliniana Library appear less edited, especially for grammar and spelling. In the case of Louisa Davis, I found additional biographical information from her interview, which I included in brackets. Also, the South Caroliniana Library has a photo of her. Both the Library of Congress and the South Caroliniana Library have a second interview of Richard Mack by a different person. I did not include this interview.

Wade Hampton's Black Red Shirts

1. Lucille Mears Poinsette, interview with the author and Eugene C. Hunt, April 2, 1981, and photograph of Wade Hampton's followers, both in Avery Research Center, College of Charleston, Charleston, S.C.; George Brown Tindall, *South Carolina Negroes,*

1877–1900 (Columbia: University of South Carolina Press, 1970), 66. Poinsette showed me the ebony cane.

2. Thomas Holt, *Black over White: Negro Political Leadership in South Carolina during Reconstruction* (Urbana: University of Illinois Press, 1979), 3. Ironically, Holt also argued that important black Republican leaders in South Carolina were bourgeois and often did not act in the interests of black peasants.

For a discussion of black Democrats in Charleston and their support of Hampton, see Bernard E. Powers Jr., *Black Charlestonians: A Social History, 1822–1885* (Fayetteville: University of Arkansas Press, 1994), 123, 174–75, 244–45. For Riley, see Powers, *Black Charlestonians,* 168, 175, 224. Powers noted that after the municipal election of 1868, a mob of black Republicans, failing to capture Riley, damaged his stables. Richard Mack's interviewer asked him about Riley. See Slave Narratives, vol. 14, pt. 3: 155–56.

An account of the Hibernian meeting may be found in the Charleston *Journal of Commerce,* October 28, 1876. For conservatives calling on Federal troops, see Alfred B. Williams, *Hampton and His Red Shirts: South Carolina's Deliverance in 1876* (Charleston, S.C.: Walker, Evans and Cogswell Co., 1935), 120–21; *Columbia Daily Union-Herald,* September 8, 1876.

For works on free blacks in Charleston, see Willard B. Gatewood, *Aristocrats of Color: The Black Elite, 1880–1920* (Bloomington: Indiana University Press, 1990), and the bibliography in Edmund L. Drago, *Initiative, Paternalism, and Race Relations: Charleston's Avery Normal Institute* (Athens: University of Georgia, 1990), 359–84. The best account of Republican factionalism in Charleston remains William C. Hine, "Frustration, Factionalism, and Failure: Black Political Leadership and the Republican Party in Reconstruction Charleston, 1865–1877" (Ph.D. diss., Kent State University, 1978). See also Hine, "Black Politicians in Reconstruction Charleston, South Carolina," *Journal of Southern History* 49 (November 1983): 555–84.

3. For traditional accounts, see William Watts Ball, *A Boy's Recollections of the Red Shirt Campaign of 1876 in South Carolina: Paper Read before the Kosmos Club of Columbia, S.C.* (Columbia: State Co., 1911), and Ball, *The State that Forgot: South Carolina's Surrender to Democracy* (Indianapolis: Bobbs-Merrill, 1932); Hampton M. Jarrell, *Wade Hampton and the Negro: The Road Not Taken* (Columbia: University of South Carolina Press, 1950); John S. Reynolds, *Reconstruction in South Carolina, 1865–1877* (Columbia: State Co., 1905; reprint, New York: Negro Universities Press, 1969); William Arthur Sheppard, *Red Shirts Remembered: Southern Brigadiers of the Reconstruction Period* (Atlanta: Ruralist Press, 1940); Henry T. Thompson, *Ousting the Carpetbagger from South Carolina* (Columbia: R. L. Bryan Co., 1927); Manly Wade Wellman, *Giant in Gray: A Biography of Wade Hampton of South Carolina* (New York: Charles Scribner's Sons, 1949); Williams, *Hampton and His Red Shirts.* Jarrell mentioned Delany only once in *Wade Hampton and the Negro* (69).

For revisionist accounts, see Holt, *Black over White*; Peggy Lamson, *The Glorious Failure: Black Congressman Robert Brown Elliot and the Reconstruction in South Carolina* (New York: W. W. Norton and Co., Norton Library, 1973); Francis Butler Simkins and Robert Hilliard Woody, *South Carolina during Reconstruction* (Chapel Hill: University of

North Carolina Press, 1932); Lou Falkner Williams, *The Great South Carolina Ku Klux Klan Trials, 1871–1872* (Athens: University of Georgia Press, 1996); Williamson, *After Slavery*; Richard Zuczek, *State of Rebellion: Reconstruction in South Carolina* (Columbia: University of South Carolina Press, 1996).

Historians have also given short shrift to black Democratic canvassers or stump speakers such as John Lee of Richland County, S. L. Hutchens of Richland County, and Richard Roman of Abbeville County. In *Hampton and His Red Shirts,* Williams named local black Democratic leaders such as Richard Roman and Aaron Mitchell, also from Abbeville County (363), but the index did not list them (456, 458). Of more significance, Williams did not identify Mitchell as a Red Shirt. See *South Carolina in 1876,* 1 (Serial 1727): 587–96 (Lee), 600–609 (Hutchens), 954–57 (Roman), 962–70 (Mitchell).

In *Been in the Storm So Long,* Litwack demonstrated how the black experience was not monolithic. See Leon F. Litwack, *Been in the Storm So Long: The Aftermath of Slavery* (New York: Alfred A. Knopf, 1979). In *Deromanticizing Black History,* Walker noted that blacks were hardly a monolithic group; some took a decidedly conservative path. See Clarence E. Walker, *Deromanticizing Black History: Critical Essays and Reappraisals* (Knoxville: University of Tennessee Press, 1991).

Historians have recognized the conservatism of the peasantry in other countries. According to Peter Kolchin, some Soviet scholars noted such conservatism in Russian peasants who remained loyal to the tsar. See Kolchin, *Unfree Labor: American Slavery and Russian Serfdom* (Cambridge, Mass.: Belknap Press of Harvard University Press, 1987), 239–40.

For an analysis of the campaign of 1876 as a counterrevolution, see Jarrell, *Wade Hampton and the Negro,* 41. On Delany, see Drago, *Initiative, Paternalism, and Race Relations,* 65; Holt, *Black over White,* 75, 176, 211; Williams, *Hampton and His Red Shirts,* 222.

4. For a critique of "agency," see Peter Coclanis, "Review Essay: Slavery, African-American Agency, and the World We Have Lost," *Georgia Historical Quarterly* 79 (Winter 1995): 873–84. Jarrell, *Wade Hampton and the Negro,* jacket biography; Donna Olendorf, ed., *Contemporary Authors* (Detroit: Gale Research, 1994), 144: 487; Zuczek, *State of Rebellion,* 168–69, 183; Williamson, *After Slavery,* 409–11. The "carpetbag correspondent" for the *New York Times* whom Williamson cited was probably James G. Thompson, editor of the Republican *Columbia Daily Union-Herald.* See Columbia *Daily Union-Herald,* October 17, 1876. Simkins and Woody, *South Carolina during Reconstruction,* 564–69 (appendix), includes Gary's "Plan of the Campaign of 1876"; see rule no. 21 on 567–68.

5. Slave Narratives, vol. 14, pt. 1: 76.

6. Simkins and Woody, *South Carolina during Reconstruction,* 567–68; *Abbeville Medium,* August 30, September 6, 1876.

7. See traditional and revisionist accounts mentioned in note 3 above.

8. *South Carolina in 1876,* vols. 1 and 2 (Serial 1728). See chart sources, note 2, for the names of the specific individuals testifying.

9. Slave Narratives, South Carolina, vol. 14, pts. 1–4, in WPA Collection, Library

of Congress; Slave Narratives, George Fleming, in WPA Federal Writers' Project Papers, South Caroliniana Library; *Columbia State*, September 24, 28, 1911.

See chart sources, note 1, for the names of the black Red Shirts identified in the slave narratives. Some of the black Red Shirts listed in the chart might have been involved in the Hampton campaign of 1878 instead of the campaign of 1876, or they may have been involved in both. For examples, see the narratives of Ed Barber and Andy Brice. Also see Tindall, *South Carolina Negroes*, 33–34.

This list does not include at least ten other blacks who may have been perceived as Red Shirts. The *Abbeville Medium*, September 20, 1876, described Marion Wilson, "the ensign, bearing aloft a beautiful banner" and marching with the "Tilden and Hendricks colored Club of Abbeville" in a Hampton procession. Richard Roman (Abbeville County) and Ouillah Harrison (Fairfield County), both mentioned in the text, are other examples. On October 13, 1876, at a Democratic rally in Due West, "Capt. Neal Richey, the first local black to declare for Hampton, led the Due West colored Democratic club in the grand parade." See Lowry Ware, *A Place Called Due West: The Home of Erskine College* (N.p.: R. L. Bryan Co., 1997), 107.

10. Joel D. Treese, ed., *Biographical Directory of the American Congress, 1774–1996* (Alexandria, Va.: CQ Staff Directories, 1997), 770, 812, 1513–14; *South Carolina in 1876*, 1: 213.

11. The narratives be must be approached with caution. For example, see how differently Susan Hamlin was interviewed, first by a white woman (Jessie A. Butler), then by a black man (Augustus Ladson), in Slave Narratives, vol. 14, pt. 2: 223–36. See Paul D. Escott, "The Art and Science of Reading WPA Slave Narratives," in *Slave Narratives*, ed. Charles T. Davis and Henry Louis Gates Jr. (New York: Oxford University Press, 1985), 40–48. For identification of interviewers' race, see Escott's *Slavery Remembered: A Record of Twentieth-Century Slave Narratives* (Chapel Hill: University of North Carolina Press, 1979), 188.

The comments of WPA appraisers also reveal some of the problems in interpreting these narratives. WPA appraiser H. Bennett ridiculed W. W. Dixon's rendering of the dialect as "exaggerated" and "likely to appeal to a reader interested in the traditional comedy Negro of the Old South." See Appraisal Sheets, Frank Adamson, Charley Barber, Andy Brice, John C. Brown and Adeline Brown, and Thomas Campbell.

The difficulties dialect pose in transcribing the narratives become apparent when comparing those at the Library of Congress with their counterparts at the South Caroliniana Library. Charley Barber's interview is an example. On pt. 1, p. 36, of the Library of Congress document, the typed word "de" is inserted. In the South Caroliniana Library version, the typed word "the" instead of "de" is inserted in the same location.

Furthermore, the narratives are rich in dialect in striking contrast to the testimonies. Yet the interviewees in both collections came from similar backgrounds. Many of them were poor, illiterate ex-slaves engaged in farming.

For Ed Barber, see Slave Narratives, vol. 14, pt. 1: 34, 36.

12. Slave Narratives, vol. 14, pt. 1: 13, 75, 77; Hugo A. Pearce Jr., ed., *The Citadel*

Alumni Directory Comprising a Register of Graduates from 1842 to 1959 and Non-Graduate Members of the Association ([Charleston, S.C.]: Association of Citadel Men, 1960), 157; William Woodward Dixon, Standard Certificate of Death, no. 11829 (filed October 9, 1944, Fairfield County), South Carolina Department of Archives and History (hereafter cited as SCDAH), Columbia. The certificate states that Dixon died on October 1, 1944, and that his father was Samuel Lee Dixon. For W. W. Dixon's obituary, see *Winnsboro Fairfield News and Herald,* October 5, 1944.

13. W. W. Dixon's grandfather, Tillman Lee Dixon, was a third cousin of Thomas Dixon's father. See W. W. Dixon, "Facts about Fairfield," March 19, 1936, in scrapbook of W. W. Dixon articles, Fairfield Genealogy Room, Fairfield County Museum, Winnsboro, S.C.; Slave Narratives, vol. 14, pt. 1: 172–75; Thomas Dixon Jr., *The Clansman: An Historical Romance of the Ku Klux Klan* (New York: Doubleday, Page and Co., 1905). In a description of the leading characters in *The Clansman,* Ben Cameron is the Grand Dragon of the Klan.

14. Allen W. Trelease, *White Terror: The Ku Klux Klan Conspiracy and Southern Reconstruction* (New York: Harper and Row, 1971), 224, 353.

15. Slave Narratives, vol. 14, pt. 1: 34–37. Barber told Dixon: "You say it was '78 'stead of '76, dat day in de pines when you was dere? Well! Well! I sho' been thinkin' all dis time it was '76."

16. Compare Andy Brice's recollection of his participation in the 1878 election in Woodward, Slave Narratives, vol. 14, pt. 1: 75–79, with W. W. Dixon's own account, "The Eleventh of Our Interesting Sketches of Fairfield Citizens," October 17, 1919, scrapbook of W. W. Dixon articles. In his article, Dixon mentioned Andy Brice as a black Democrat so full of liquor that he slept peacefully throughout the whole affair. Furthermore, Dixon romanticized the Red Shirts as a white citizenship that has disappeared. His appreciation for the black Red Shirts grew as he interviewed them.

17. Slave Narratives, vol. 14, pt. 1: 151–56.

18. Simkins and Woody, *South Carolina during Reconstruction,* 480–85.

19. Ibid., 485–87; Williamson, *After Slavery,* 267–70; *Columbia Daily Union-Herald,* July 12, 1876; Williams, *Hampton and His Red Shirts,* 30.

20. Simkins and Woody, *South Carolina during Reconstruction,* 487–91, 499–500; Williamson, *After Slavery,* 268–70; *Columbia Daily Union-Herald,* July 8, 15, 1876.

21. *Greenville Enterprise and Mountaineer,* September 6, 1876.

22. Simkins and Woody, *South Carolina during Reconstruction,* 491, 500, 509–11; Tindall, *South Carolina Negroes,* 11–14; Alfred Brockenbrough Williams Scrapbook, 1926, South Caroliniana Library. While Tindall saw Gary's position as fanatical in contrast to the moderate stance of Hampton, Sheppard defended Gary as the "Bald Eagle." However, Wellman criticized Sheppard for making Hampton villainous and Gary heroic (Wellman, *Giant in Gray,* 370). As for Jarrell, the state could have avoided turmoil if it had taken the path of balance and sanity which Hampton advised (Jarrell, *Wade Hampton and the Negro,* book jacket). In contrast, Zuczek described Hampton's efforts to win black support as halfhearted (Zuczek, *State of Rebellion,* 166). For another

assessment of Hampton, see Richard Mark Gergel, "Wade Hampton and the Rise of One Party Racial Orthodoxy in South Carolina," in *The Proceedings of the South Carolina Historical Association, 1977*, ed. James O. Farmer Jr. (Lancaster: South Carolina Historical Association, 1977), 5–16.

23. Simkins and Woody, *South Carolina during Reconstruction*, 564–69; *South Carolina in 1876*, 1: 528–30, 535–37; *Abbeville Medium*, August 30, 1876; Slave Narratives, vol. 14, pt. 1: 299–300; William J. Cooper Jr., *The Conservative Regime: South Carolina, 1877–1890* (Baltimore: Johns Hopkins University Press, 1968), 22; Zuczek, *State of Rebellion*, and his article "The Last Campaign of the Civil War: South Carolina and the Revolution of 1876," *Civil War History* 42 (March 1996): 18–31. Cooper makes the military analogy, but Zuczek goes one step further by presenting the election of 1876 as the last campaign of the Civil War, even comparing Hampton's procession throughout the state with Sherman's march. In *State of Rebellion*, Zuczek dismisses the black Democratic and rifle clubs as few in number (169), and he hardly mentions them in "The Last Campaign." However, he could have incorporated them into his thesis as black auxiliaries, which is how black Red Shirts such as Richard Mack and Joe O'Bannon viewed themselves.

24. Williamson, *After Slavery*, 266–67; Zuczek, *State of Rebellion*, 169–170, and his "The Last Campaign," 22–23.

25. Simkins and Woody, *South Carolina during Reconstruction*, 501; *South Carolina in 1876*, 3: 508–9. There were more clubs because there were no statistics on the clubs from five counties. See "Rifle Clubs," folder 28–181–15, Connor Family Papers, South Carolina Historical Society (hereafter cited as SCHS), Charleston.

26. Cooper, *Conservative Regime*, 22; Walhalla (Oconee County) *Keowee Courier*, October 5, 1876.

27. D. S. Henderson, "Red Shirt Revolution Told by a Participant," *Columbia State*, September 22, 1911.

28. Williams, *Hampton and His Red Shirts*, 105, 133; D. S. Henderson, "Red Shirt Revolution"; Simkins and Woody, *Reconstruction in South Carolina*, 499; U[lysses]. R. Brooks, ed., *Stories of the Confederacy* (Columbia, S.C.: State Co., 1912), 370–71. According to Brooks, the first time the red shirts were worn as a uniform was on August 12 at Edgefield when Chamberlain spoke. However, the *Charleston News and Courier*, August 14, 15, 16, 1876, did not mention red shirts in its reporting on the event.

29. *Charleston News and Courier*, September 7, 1876, described an Aiken meeting (held on September 5) that included "Col. A. P. Butler's 'bloody shirts' company" wearing "large homespun shirts stained with red paint." See also the Republican *Columbia Daily Union-Herald*, September 7, 1876; *Pickens Sentinel*, September 14, 1876.

30. John B. Edmunds Jr., *Francis W. Pickens and the Politics of Destruction* (Chapel Hill: University of North Carolina Press, 1986), 151; John Cheves Haskell Papers, Southern Historical Collection, University of North Carolina, Chapel Hill; C. Vann Woodward, ed., *Mary Chesnut's Civil War* (New Haven: Yale University Press, 1981), 282; John F. Marszalek, ed., *The Diary of Miss Emma Holmes, 1861–1866* (Baton Rouge: Louisiana

State University Press, 1994), 248; Judith N. McArthur and Orville Vernon Burton, eds., *"A Gentleman and an Officer": A Military and Social History of James B. Griffin's Civil War* (New York: Oxford University Press, 1996), 307n. 17; Jarrell, *Wade Hampton and the Negro,* 70; Wellman, *Giant in Gray,* 245, 359. Wellman saw a connection between the red shirt of 1876 and the red shirt worn by Garibaldi's followers, while Jarrell did not.

31. Simkins and Woody, *South Carolina during Reconstruction,* 568–69.

32. Williams, *Hampton and His Red Shirts,* 255–56.

33. Thompson, *Ousting the Carpetbagger,* 118.

34. Simkins and Woody, *South Carolina during Reconstruction,* 499n. 59.

35. Ball, *Boy's Recollections,* 10–11, 15, 21–22; Reynolds, *Reconstruction in South Carolina,* 359; Thompson, *Ousting the Carpetbagger,* 118–19; *Newberry Herald,* September 20, 1876.

36. Reynolds, *Reconstruction in South Carolina,* 357–58; Henderson, "Red Shirt Revolution." At a 1911 Red Shirt reunion in Columbia, Henderson described the election as "the Rise of the White Tide" that engulfed the Palmetto state, taking with it "the rich and poor alike."

37. *Abbeville Medium,* September 20, 1876; Williams, *Hampton and his Red Shirts,* 166, 201–3; Ball, *Boy's Recollections,* 5, 11–12. Ball remembered that his grandmother made him a red calico shirt and carried him, at age seven and along with a cousin, to a friend's house to see Hampton's cavalcade enter their village. To attract women, children, elderly citizens, and blacks, the men in charge of the cavalcades and processions had to maintain discipline.

38. Simkins and Woody, *South Carolina during Reconstruction,* 510, 564–69.

39. *Columbia Daily Union-Herald,* August 9, 1876. Kershaw had genuine credentials as a moderate. In 1874 President Ulysses S. Grant had considered supporting the former Confederate general for governor. See Simkins and Woody, *South Carolina during Reconstruction,* 489; Williamson, *After Slavery,* 400n. 105.

40. Jarrell, *Wade Hampton and the Negro,* 53–54, 54n. 41, 67–68. According to Jarrell, Hampton and the Democratic State Executive Committee rejected the Gary plan. For Haskell's invitation and Chamberlain's response, see *Columbia Daily Union-Herald,* October 5, 1876.

41. G. Wayne King, *Rise Up So Early: A History of Florence County* (Spartanburg, S.C.: Reprint Co., 1981), 74–75.

42. *Columbia Register,* November 6, 1876.

43. Slave Narratives, vol. 14, pt. 2: 27–29. The church was the Lower Fairforest Baptist Church.

44. Hagood was one of the first white men in South Carolina to accept testimonies by blacks on the witness stand. The former Confederate general had also supported plans for a fusionist ticket with Governor Chamberlain heading it. See Williamson, *After Slavery,* 328; Sheppard, *Red Shirts Remembered,* 65–66; Johnson Hagood, *Memoirs of the War of Secession* (Columbia, S.C.: State Co., 1910; republished Camden, S.C.: J. J. Fox, 1989), 19–20; Zuczek, *State of Rebellion,* 171; *South Carolina in 1876,* 1: 528–29, 535, 903–5.

45. *Abbeville Medium,* August 30, September 6, 1876; Slave Narratives, vol. 14, pt. 3: 194–96; pt. 1: 29, 31.

46. *Charleston News and Courier,* October 10, 1876.

47. Slave Narratives, vol. 14, pt. 2: 27–29.

48. *Abbeville Medium,* October 18, 1876.

49. Slave Narratives, vol. 14, pt. 1: 13, 15.

50. Ibid., 151–56.

51. *Columbia State,* September 24, 1911.

52. Ibid.

53. Slave Narratives, vol. 14, pt. 1: 151–56; A. S. Salley Jr., comp., *South Carolina Troops in Confederate Service* (Columbia, S.C.: R. L. Bryan Co., 1913), 1: 431–32, 452, 707–8; Index to Memory Rolls (Post–Civil War List of South Carolina Confederate Veterans), SCDAH. Since Frank Bamberg and his brother Isaac were from Barnwell County, which was adjacent to Orangeburg County where Cherry came from, the contingent of black Red Shirts Mack led could have included O'Bannon and other Barnwell black Red Shirts.

54. C. M. Douglas, "A Notable Colored Veteran," *Confederate Veteran* 2 (August 1894): 233. After the war, Rose remained associated with the Richland Volunteers, parading with them and attending Confederate reunions.

55. Patrick McCawley, *Guide to Civil War Records: A Guide to the Records in the South Carolina Department of Archives and History* (Columbia: SCDAH, 1994), 15–16. McCawley gave the author this number in a phone conversation, February 2, 1995.

56. Richard Rollins, ed., *Black Southerners in Gray: Essays on Afro-Americans in Confederate Armies, Journal of Confederate History* Series, vol. 11 (Murfreesboro, Tenn.: Southern Heritage Press, 1994), 16–17.

57. Slave Narratives, vol. 14, pt. 1: 75–79.

58. *Abbeville Medium,* July 12, August 23, 1876; *Walhalla Keowee Courier,* September 21, 1876; *Charleston News and Courier,* October 2, 1876; Williams, *Hampton and His Red Shirts,* 358.

59. Slave Narratives, vol. 14, pt. 1: 37.

60. Williams, *Hampton and His Red Shirts,* 218–19.

61. Slave Narratives, vol. 14, pt. 1: 34–35.

62. *Columbia Daily Union Herald,* September 19, 1876.

63. Lacy K. Ford Jr., *Origins of Southern Radicalism: The South Carolina Upcountry, 1800–1860* (New York: Oxford University Press, 1988), 44–48. According to Ford, the Upper Piedmont counties were Anderson, Greenville, Lancaster, Pickens, Spartanburg, and York. The Lower Piedmont included Abbeville, Chester, Edgefield, Fairfield, Laurens, Newberry, and Union.

64. Williams, *Ku Klux Klan Trials,* 19–20, 23. Williams noted that Klan outrages were common in nine counties: five in the Lower Piedmont (Chester, Fairfield, Laurens, Newberry, Union), three in the Upper Piedmont (Lancaster, Spartanburg, York), and one in the Sand Hills (Chesterfield). The population was nearly evenly divided between

whites and blacks in eight of these counties. Spartanburg, with a huge majority of whites, was the exception. According to Williams, whites in that county were bitterly opposed to any black participation in politics.

65. *South Carolina in 1876*, 1: 310; 3 (Serial 1729): 578 (Official Returns).

66. *South Carolina in 1876*, 1: 270, 445, 448–49; *Abbeville Medium*, July 12, 1876; *Columbia Daily Union-Herald*, July 7, August 8, 1876. Actually, the *Medium* was alluding to a Republican rally at Calhoun's Mills (a voting precinct) called by the white Republican sheriff L. P. Guffin. A number of the whites present were from Georgia.

67. *Abbeville Medium*, July 5, 1876.

68. C. A. Mathison to D. H. Chamberlain, August 1, 1876, Daniel H. Chamberlain Papers, SCDAH.

69. A. Blythe to D. H. Chamberlain, September 19, 1876, Chamberlain Papers.

70. Benj. F. Moore to D. H. Chamberlain, November 1, 1876, Chamberlain Papers.

71. Richard Mark Zuczek, "State of Rebellion: People's War in Reconstruction South Carolina, 1865–1877" (Ph.D. diss., Ohio State University, 1993), 199.

72. S. G. Welch to D. H. Chamberlain, August 23, 1876, Chamberlain Papers.

73. Benj. F. Moore to D. H. Chamberlain, November 1, 1876, Chamberlain Papers. According to Joel Williamson, Republicans in Laurens, Chester, and Newberry Counties used their positions as election managers in 1870 to pad the black vote. One of the worst offenders was the former slave trader Joseph Crews of Laurens County. See Williamson, *After Slavery*, 347–48.

74. *Columbia Daily Union-Herald*, July 11, 1876.

75. Sheppard, *Red Shirts Remembered*, 65–71, 128.

76. *Abbeville Medium*, September 13, 1876.

77. Sheppard, *Red Shirts Remembered*, 71–77; *Charleston News and Courier*, May 25, 26, 27, 1876.

78. *Abbeville Medium*, July 19, 1876.

79. *Columbia Daily Union-Herald*, August 4, 5, 8, 1876.

80. *Columbia Daily Union-Herald*, August 8, 1876.

81. *New York Herald* as cited in the *Columbia Daily Union-Herald*, July 29, 1876. One of the reasons the Federal government agreed to take the troops out of the South was the need to deal with the Indians in the West.

82. *Columbia Daily Union-Herald*, October 21, 1876.

83. *South Carolina in 1876*, 1: 432, 436–37.

84. *Abbeville Medium*, August 23, 1876.

85. *Abbeville Medium*, September 27, 1876.

86. *Abbeville Medium*, September 6, 1876.

87. *Abbeville Medium*, November 8, 1876.

88. *Abbeville Medium*, September 13, 1876.

89. Williams, *Hampton and His Red Shirts*, 174; Lowry Ware, *Old Abbeville: Scenes of the Past of a Town Where Old Time Things Are Not Forgotten* (Columbia, S.C.: SCMAR,

1992), 231-32. According to Ware, Parker was first elected intendant in 1869. Aaron Mitchell describes him as a lawyer in *South Carolina in 1876*, 1: 964.

90. *Abbeville Medium*, September 27, 1876.

91. Williams, *Hampton and His Red Shirts*, 151; *Marion Star*, October 11, 1876.

92. *Abbeville Medium*, September 13, 1876.

93. *Abbeville Medium*, October 25, 1876.

94. *Abbeville Medium*, September 20, 27, 1876.

95. *Abbeville Medium*, October 25, 1876.

96. *South Carolina in 1876*, 2: 367–70; 3: 499; *Abbeville Medium*, September 20, October 4, 1876. In an official government document Young and Peak[e] were listed as captains of the Lowndesville and Bordeaux rifle clubs respectively.

97. Abbeville *Medium*, October 18, 1876.

98. *South Carolina in 1876*, 2: 211, 369.

99. *Abbeville Medium*, August 9; September 27, 1876.

100. *South Carolina in 1876*, 1: 958–62.

101. Ibid., 954–55; *Abbeville Medium*, October 18, 1876; Williamson, *After Slavery*, 385–88. According to revisionist Joel Williamson, the Philadelphia financier John J. Patterson was an associate of railroad magnate Thomas A. Scott, and a friend of the merchant-banker Hardy Solomon. Patterson, who had bought his seat in the United States Senate, subsequently helped get legislation passed that paid Solomon the debt the state owed him.

Thomas E. Miller, a black Republican lawyer from Beaufort who served as a state legislator and U.S. congressman during Reconstruction, supported Roman's claims of Republican corruption. According to Miller, Chamberlain, ignoring the protest of black Republican Francis L. Cardozo, placed in Hardy Solomon's bank the state funds, part of which he used to assure his nomination in September 1876. Miller believed that if South Carolinians had heeded Hampton's advice after he was elected governor, racial radicalism would not have succeeded. See Thomas E. Miller to Respected Sir [Theodore D. Jervey], December 19, 1927, folder 28–248–15, Theodore D. Jervey Papers, SCHS, as cited in *Carologue* 12 (Winter 1996): 13. See also in the same issue, William C. Hine, "Thomas E. Miller and the Early Years of South Carolina State University," 8–12.

102. *Abbeville Medium*, October 4, 1876.

103. *Abbeville Medium*, November 8, 1876; *South Carolina in 1876*, 1: 955.

104. The three brothers held many offices: Lemuel L. (L. L. or "Lem") Guffin (magistrate, county auditor, judge of probate, legislator); Lawrence P. (L. P. or "Pem") Guffin (county commissioner, legislator, sheriff); Charles W. (C. W. or "Will") Guffin (intendant or mayor of Abbeville). According to hearsay, Mitchell was removed from office because he allowed two blacks to fight "in the corporate limits, upon payment of the sum of $5." The staunchly conservative *Abbeville Press and Banner* defended the blacksmith: "We trust our former Marshal is only under a temporary cloud and that he will come out again in noon-day splendor." Mitchell, Edward Henderson, and Asbury

Green mentioned the Guffins in their testimonies. Green sang the Democratic song "We'll hang Lem Guffin on a hickory tree" to the tune of John Brown. See *South Carolina in 1876,* 1: 270, 315, 940, 959, 962–70; *Abbeville Medium,* November 15, 1876; *Abbeville Press and Banner,* March 3, April 28, 1871; Ware, *Old Abbeville,* 121, 124, 139, 231; Lowry Ware to Edmund L. Drago, July 22, 1997.

According to Ware, "the most prominent of the scalawags" in Abbeville were the Guffins and Tolberts. But many local whites shared Mitchell's particular antipathy for the Guffins. Tom Lomax mentioned the Tolberts in his testimony. See *South Carolina in 1876,* 2: 212, 213.

105. *South Carolina in 1876,* 1: 962–70; chart. According to the 1870 Federal census, Mitchell could read but not write.

106. *Abbeville Medium,* September 20, 1876.

107. *Abbeville Medium,* September 27, 1876.

108. *Abbeville Medium,* October 18, 1876.

109. *Abbeville Medium,* November 1, 1876.

110. *South Carolina in 1876,* 1: 969.

111. Chart; *Abbeville Medium,* September 6, 13, 20, 1876; *South Carolina in 1876,* 1: 938–40, 954; Ware, *Old Abbeville,* 39. According to Ware, Henderson's unit wore blue shirts while rural whites dressed in red shirts.

112. Abbeville *Medium,* September 6, October 4, 1876; *South Carolina in 1876,* 2: 211–14.

113. *South Carolina in 1876,* 1: 938.

114. Glenn C. Altschuler and Stuart M. Blumin, "Limits of Political Engagement in Antebellum America: A New Look at the Golden Age of Participatory Democracy," *Journal of American History* 84 (December 1997): 873.

115. *Charleston News and Courier,* September 8, 1876.

116. Ibid.

117. Ibid.; *Abbeville Medium,* September 20, 1876.

118. *Charleston News and Courier,* October 5, 1876.

119. Williams Scrapbook; Williams, *Hampton and His Red Shirts,* 244–45.

120. *Charleston News and Courier,* October 10, 1876.

121. *Greenville Enterprise and Mountaineer,* October 19, 1876.

122. Williams Scrapbook; Williams, *Hampton and His Red Shirts,* 290.

123. Williams Scrapbook; Williams, *Hampton and His Red Shirts,* 316.

124. Williams Scrapbook; Williams, *Hampton and His Red Shirts,* 323–24.

125. Williams Scrapbook; Williams, *Hampton and His Red Shirts,* 325, 328–29.

126. Clipping, *Charleston News and Courier,* October 31, 1876, in Reconstruction Scrapbook, South Caroliniana Library.

127. *Charleston News and Courier,* November 3, 1876.

128. *Columbia Daily Union-Herald,* September 13, 1876.

129. Lamson, *Glorious Failure,* 202.

130. *Columbia Daily Union-Herald,* October 17, 1876. Citing the *New York Times,* October 21 and October 29, 1876, Joel Williamson stated that a carpetbag journalist,

attending a Red Shirt parade in Edgefield in October, counted 9 blacks among the 1,600 mounted men in contrast to the 200 claimed by the Democratic press. See Williamson, *After Slavery,* 411n. 132, 409n. 126; Williams, *Hampton and His Red Shirts,* 307. Citing Williamson, Zuczek repeated similar numbers in *State of the Rebellion,* 169, 183n. 56.

The carpetbag journalist was probably the partisan Republican editor of the *Columbia Daily-Union Herald,* James G. Thompson. He doubled as a correspondent for the *Times.* See Thompson's testimony in *South Carolina in 1876,* 2: 483–88.

131. Ralph E. Evans to D. H. Chamberlain, September 30, 1876, Chamberlain Papers.

132. *Columbia Daily Union-Herald,* October 21, 1876.

133. *Columbia Daily Union-Herald,* November 4, 1876.

134. *Columbia Daily Union-Herald,* November 1, 1876.

135. *Columbia Daily Union-Herald,* October 27, 1976.

136. *Columbia Daily Union-Herald,* November 4, 1876.

137. *Columbia Daily Union-Herald,* October 21, 1876.

138. *South Carolina in 1876,* 1: 958.

139. Residence, 1865–1880, is used to determine counties.

140. Ford, *Origins of Southern Radicalism,* 45–47.

141. Slave Narratives, George Fleming.

142. Slave Narratives, vol. 14, pt. 2: 212–14.

143. Slave Narratives, vol. 14, pt. 1: 13–16; Julian Stevenson Bolick, *A Fairfield Sketchbook* (Clinton, S.C.: Jacobs Bros., c. 1963), 43.

144. Slave Narratives, vol. 14, pt. 1: 176–79; Bolick, *A Fairfield Sketchbook,* 84, 86.

145. Slave Narratives, vol. 14, pt. 1: 299–303.

146. Slave Narratives, Martha Lowery, folder labeled "Questionable," container A907, Library of Congress. For a study of black conservatism and religion in another state, see Edmund L. Drago, *Black Politicians and Reconstruction in Georgia: A Splendid Failure* (Athens: University of Georgia Press, Brown Thrasher edition, 1992).

147. See chart.

148. Minute Book, 1876–1880, August 31, September 21, October 5, 1876, Richland Democratic Club, Columbia, South Caroliniana Library.

149. George C. Rogers Jr., "Who Is a South Carolinian?" *South Carolina Historical Magazine* 89 (January 1988), 3–12; Williamson, *After Slavery,* 361; *New York Times,* August 9, 1867. According to Williamson, given a choice between a white Northerner or a white South Carolinian, the former slaves would usually elect the latter.

150. Davie wrote that he would vote for the general and recruit other blacks because he owned some land in York County and that he needed good laws and taxes in order to support his family. The *Columbia Register,* September 20, 1876, reported that Hampton read this letter at an Abbeville rally on September 16, 1876. Also see Wellman, *Giant in Gray,* 257–58.

151. *South Carolina in 1876,* 1: 555–56, 560–65; Merimon Washington, Lower Township, Richland Co., S.C., Dwelling No. 640, House No. 672, p. 361 (Roll 1238) in 1880 MSS Census, Population Schedules (Microfilm Series T9), National Archives, Washington,

D.C. *Abbeville Medium,* September 27, 1876, reported that a number of blacks were naming their "boy babies" after Hampton.

152. See table 1 and chart; *South Carolina in 1876,* 1: 970; Slave Narratives, vol. 14, pt. 2: 27–29, 212–14.

153. See chart; *South Carolina in 1876,* 1: 561, 940, 969–70. The four found in the 1870 census were Fleming, Mitchell, O'Bannon, and Weeks.

154. See chart.

155. Slave Narratives, vol. 14, pt. 1: 34–37.

156. Ibid., 127–30.

157. Ware, *Old Abbeville,* 36–39; *South Carolina in 1876,* 1: 938–40; Edward Henderson, Abbeville, Abbeville Co., SC, Dwelling No. 33, Family No. 53, p. 3 (Roll 1217), 1880 MSS Census.

158. Slave Narratives, vol. 14, pt. 1: 75–79, 172; see chart. The sample may be influenced by the fact that the older black Red Shirts had passed away by 1937 when the slave narratives were taken. An exception is Richard Mack, who was 104 years old when he was interviewed.

159. See chart sources, n. 2.

160. Slave Narratives, vol. 14, pt. 2: 247–51. Harvey identified his parents as Tom and Mandy Clark of Union County. His uncles Jipp and Charlie Clark were in Stonewall Jackson's brigade. He might have been referring to the Klan of the 1920s, but the reference to Scott suggested he was referring to Reconstruction times. Conservatives blamed the Klan on the governor's arming of the black militia. See Simkins and Woody, *South Carolina during Reconstruction,* 452.

161. Slave Narratives, vol. 14, pt. 2: 212, 214.

162. Slave Narratives, vol. 14, 1: 75–79.

163. Slave Narratives, George Fleming; Simkins and Woody, *South Carolina during Reconstruction,* 128; Michael Tadman, *Speculators and Slaves: Masters, Traders, and Slaves in the Old South* (Madison: University of Wisconsin Press, 1989), 195–96.

164. *The Ku Klux Conspiracy: Testimony Taken by the Joint Select Committee to Inquire into the Condition of Affairs in the Late Insurrectionary States* (Washington: Government Printing Office, 1872), vols. 3–5 of 13 vols. deal with South Carolina (cited as SC vols. 1–3). See SC vol. 1: xi (index) for "Fleming, William, a colored man, killed in the Laurens riot, 1149, 1313." For accounts of the riot, see testimonies by Joe Crews's son John, SC vol. 2: 1144–55, and Democratic lawyer William D. Simpson, SC vol. 3: 1302–42. Although Simpson called William Fleming "Peter," John Crews, who helped his father organize the black militia, correctly identified the man. Also see Slave Narratives, George Fleming; Ball, *Boy's Recollections,* 3–5; Simkins and Woody, *South Carolina during Reconstruction,* 490.

165. Slave Narratives, George Fleming.

166. Thompson, *Ousting the Carpetbagger,* 50n. 88; Williams, *Hampton and His Red Shirts,* 48; *South Carolina in 1876,* 1: 223–24, 231. Richard T. Greener, a black Republican speaker for the 1876 campaign, informed a Congressional committee: "I really dreaded

Laurens worse than any other place, because I knew it was the place where Joe Crews had been assassinated, and where the democrats were bitter and hostile."

167. Slave Narratives, George Fleming.

168. Williams, *Ku Klux Klan Trials,* 19, 63–64; Slave Narratives, vol. 14, pt. 2: 212–14.

169. Samuel Jones to D. H. Chamberlain, August 13, 1876, Chamberlain Papers.

170. Slave Narratives, vol. 14, pt. 3: 277–79.

171. Slave Narratives, vol. 14, pt. 1: 170, 227–28; pt. 2: 136–37; Williams, *Hampton and His Red Shirts,* 267.

172. *Pickens Sentinel,* September 14, 1876.

173. That day a Camden mounted club, marching in a Sumter procession, carried a plank with a raccoon skin nailed to it to illustrate how Chamberlain would be treated. On November 4 in Columbia the Richland Rifle Club still had a banner in the Hampton parade. See Williams, *Hampton and His Red Shirts,* 244–45; *Columbia Register,* November 6, 1867.

174. Anne King Gregorie, *History of Sumter County, South Carolina* (Sumter, S.C.: Library Board of Sumter County, 1954), 347; Williams Scrapbook; Williams, *Hampton and His Red Shirts,* 246; Sheppard, *Black Shirts Remembered,* 147–48.

175. *New York Times,* October 16, 1876.

176. Lamson, *Glorious Failure,* 248; Sheppard, *Red Shirts Remembered,* 149; Woody and Simkins, *South Carolina during Reconstruction,* 508–9; Zuczek, *State of Rebellion,* 178–79, 186–87n. 120.

177. *Abbeville Medium,* November 8, 1876; *South Carolina in 1876,* 1: 315, 318–19; Jarrell, *Wade Hampton and the Negro,* 92.

178. *Abbeville Medium,* October 25, November 8, 15, 1876.

179. *Abbeville Medium,* November 8, 1876.

180. *Charleston News and Courier,* October 10, 1876.

181. *Charleston News and Courier,* October 5, 1876.

182. *Abbeville Medium,* September 20, 1876.

183. *South Carolina in 1876,* 3: 557–58.

184. *South Carolina in 1876,* 1: 936–38 (Guy Taylor, Edgefield County); 2: 72–73 (Cornelius R. Meas, Fairfield County); 2: 644–46 (Stephen Nesbitt, Laurens County).

185. *South Carolina in 1876,* 1: 600–609. On 606, although Hutchens stated he was originally from Indianapolis, Indiana, he also said that he was born in Georgia where he lived until he was ten years old.

186. Ibid., 587–88.

187. Ibid., 596–97.

188. Ibid., 962–64; see chart (1870 census).

189. *Abbeville Medium,* August 30, September 6, 27, 1876.

190. *Columbia Daily Union-Herald,* October 16, 25, 28; November 1, 2, 1876; Holt, *Black over White,* 34–35.

191. Simkins and Woody, *South Carolina during Reconstruction,* 512, briefly describes some of the militant activities by black women. They were especially active in Charleston.

A letter from a reader in Charleston to the *Columbia Daily Union-Herald*, September 13, 1876, declared: "The negro women are particularly bitter, and their temper and language is calculated to alarm the families of such democrats as are away in the evenings attending the club meetings."

For protest about "hoop skirts," see *Charleston News and Courier*, October 1, 1878. During his re-election campaign of 1878, Hampton recalled meeting with the black women in 1876 and telling them that "they could wear anything they liked, from a fig-leaf up." The audience responded with "cheers and laughter." The governor continued, "Now no women wore hoop skirts at all."

For a comparison to another state, see Edmund L. Drago, "Militancy and Black Women in Reconstruction Georgia," *Journal of American Culture* 1 (Winter 1978): 838–44.

192. *South Carolina in 1876*, 1: 954.

193. Ibid., 958–60. For the names of the family, see Asbury Green, Cokesbury Township, Abbeville County, SC, Dwelling No. 317, Family No. 341, p. 217 (Roll 1217), 1880 MSS Census. In 1876 Mary Green gave birth to a girl.

194. *South Carolina in 1876*, 1: 587, 591–93.

195. *South Carolina in 1876*, 2: 211–12.

196. Williamson, *After Slavery*, 103–4; Holt, *Black over White*, 3, 167–68. Newspapers throughout the state covered the strike. From my conversations with Elizabeth Motherwell, I gained the insight that these women treated black Democrats as white Democrats had abused black men and women.

197. Slave Narratives, George Fleming.

198. *South Carolina in 1876*, 1: 592.

199. *Ku Klux Conspiracy*, SC vol. 3: 1302, 1304.

200. Slave Narratives, vol. 14, pt. 1: 75, 77–78.

201. *South Carolina in 1876*, 1: 939.

202. Ibid., 560–62; Jonas Weeks, Lower Township, Richland Co., SC, Dwelling No. 648, Family No. 679, p. 362 (Roll 1238), 1880 MSS Census.

203. *Columbia Daily Union-Herald*, October 23, 1876.

204. *Abbeville Medium*, September 27, 1876.

205. *South Carolina in 1876*, 1: 562–63.

206. Ibid., 555–56.

207. Ibid., 962, 965–66.

208. *Abbeville Medium*, November 8, 1876.

209. *South Carolina in 1876*, 1: 938–39; Edward Henderson, Abbeville, Abbeville Co., SC, Dwelling No. 33, Family No. 53, p. 3 (Roll 1217), 1880 MSS Census. "Vote of Abbeville County at the General Election, November 7th, 1876," *Abbeville Medium*, November 15, 1876, listed Samuel McGowan as a presidential elector.

210. *Columbia Daily Union-Herald*, September 14, 1876.

211. *Abbeville Medium*, September 6, 1876.

212. *Columbia Daily Union-Herald*, November 8, 1876. Black women have often been

presented in stereotypes. See Patricia Morton, *Disfigured Images: The Historical Assault on Afro-American Women* (Westport, Conn.: Praeger, 1991).

213. Simkins and Woody, *South Carolina during Reconstruction,* 514; Jarrell, *Wade Hampton and the Negro,* 99; *South Carolina in 1876,* 1: 600–601, 605. According to S. L. Hutchens, two thousand black Democrats did not vote. For the number of white Republicans, see Williamson, *After Slavery,* 349n. 78.

214. Ball, *Boy's Recollections,* 16.

215. Williamson, *After Slavery,* 410–11.

216. Slave Narratives, Martha Lowery.

217. *Columbia Daily Union-Herald,* December 6, 1876.

218. See table 2. Obviously, if some whites voted for Chamberlain, then the percentage of black Hampton voters would have been even higher.

219. *South Carolina in 1876,* 1: 266–69.

220. Ibid., 431.

221. Ibid., 270–76 (L. P. Guffin), ibid., 315–19 (L. L. Guffin, clerk of court candidate), ibid., 327–44 (W. H. Heard, state house of representatives candidate), ibid., 432–37 (L. Clay, county commissioner candidate). For identification of candidates, see "Vote of Abbeville County."

222. Ibid., 329–30, 427, 432, 435–36.

223. Ibid., 432, 435 (L. Clay); ibid., 327, 330 (W. H. Heard); ibid., 427 (A. Titus).

224. See table 2.

225. See table 2.

226. *Abbeville Medium,* November 8, 1876; *South Carolina in 1876,* 2: 367.

227. See table 2; *South Carolina in 1876,* 1: 962–65.

228. *Abbeville Medium,* November 15, 1876; see table 2. For more, see Ware, *A Place Called Due West,* 100–108.

229. *Abbeville Medium,* November 8, 15, 22, 1876.

230. *Marion Star,* November 22, 1876.

231. *Abbeville Medium,* September 20, November 1, 1876.

232. *Marion Star,* November 22, 1876.

233. Jarrell, *Wade Hampton and the Negro,* 147–49; *Charleston News and Courier,* September 24, 1878.

234. *Charleston News and Courier,* September 14, 1878; Slave Narratives, vol. 14, pt. 1: 75–79.

235. For newspaper accounts of the black Red Shirts in Barnwell County and Gantt's case, see *Charleston News and Courier,* October 12, 28; November 7, 9, 19, 22; December 9, 10, 18, 1878; April 19, 21, 22, 23, 1879. Another account of the Blackville affair is "The United States Indictment for Conspiracy, Osceola Gantt, David White et al," dated the fourth Monday of November 1879, District of South Carolina, United States of America, Letters Received by the Department of Justice from South Carolina 1871–1884, Record Group 60, General Records of the Department of Justice Records (Microfilm

Series M947, Roll 4, July 1878–February 1879), National Archives, College Park, Md. According to the indictment, Gantt and the others "did then and there conspire with intent to do, by unlawfully and with force and arms, assaulting, threatening, cursing, abusing and using all manner of violence" to keep Frederick Nix and others from holding a peaceful meeting on behalf of black Congressional candidate Robert Smalls. For the best analysis of Democratic intimidation during the 1878 election, see Lou Falkner Williams, "The Federal Courts and the Electoral Process in Post-Reconstruction South Carolina," a paper read at the annual meeting of the Southern Historical Association in Atlanta on November 8, 1997.

236. Ware, *Old Abbeville,* 39, 164, 232; Wellman, *Giant in Gray,* 300–301; Tindall, *South Carolina Negroes,* 39; *South Carolina in 1876,* 1: 940; 2: 211. When asked if he had resorted to "any force to induce the colored people to vote the democratic ticket," Henderson asserted, "Not one word." He told the committee to check with United States Marshal Burt Griffin and William Pope, a black Presbyterian leader and former town warden (alderman).

237. Tindall, *South Carolina Negroes,* 67; Slave Narratives, vol. 14, pt. 2: 28–29.

238. B[enjamin] R. Tillman, *The Struggles of '76: Address Delivered at the Red Shirt Reunion, Anderson, S.C., August 25th, 1909* (n.p., n.d.), 28.

239. *Columbia State,* September 28, 30, 1911. Carried away by the emotions at the reunion, Blease claimed he had voted for Wade Hampton in 1890. A later article in the newspaper reminded readers that Blease eventually switched his vote at the joint assembly.

240. *Columbia State,* September 24, 28, 29, 1911.

241. Clipping, *Columbia State,* September 3, 1938, file no. 1580 (History-Reconstruction), Clipping Collection, Main Branch, Charleston County Library, Charleston, S.C.

242. Slave Narratives, vol. 14, pt. 1: 13–15.

243. Slave Narratives, vol. 14, pt. 2: 29.

NAME INDEX